JOAN MARTIN (YARRNA)

Joan Martin, courtesy Errol Martin.

JOAN MARTIN (YARRNA)
A Widi Woman

As told to Bruce Shaw

Aboriginal Studies Press

First published in 2011
by Aboriginal Studies Press

© Errol Martin and Bruce Shaw 2011

All rights reserved. No part of this book may be reproduced or transmitted in any form or by any means, electronic or mechanical, including photocopying, recording or by any information storage and retrieval system, without prior permission in writing from the publisher. The *Australian Copyright Act 1968* (the Act) allows a maximum of one chapter or 10 per cent of this book, whichever is the greater, to be photocopied by any educational institution for its education purposes provided that the educational institution (or body that administers it) has given a remuneration notice to Copyright Agency Limited (CAL) under the Act.

Aboriginal Studies Press
is the publishing arm of the
Australian Institute of Aboriginal
and Torres Strait Islander Studies.
GPO Box 553, Canberra, ACT 2601
Phone: (61 2) 6246 1183
Fax: (61 2) 6261 4288
Email: asp@aiatsis.gov.au
Web: www.aiatsis.gov.au/asp/welcome.html

National Library of Australia Cataloguing-In-Publication data:

   Author: Shaw, Bruce Clayton, 1941-

   Title: Joan Martin : a Widi woman / Bruce Shaw.

   ISBN: 9780855757779 (pbk.)
   ISBN: 9780855757496 (ebook PDF)
   ISBN: 9780855758288 (ebook ePub)
   ISBN: 9780855758295 (ebook Kindle)

   Notes: Includes bibliographical references and index.

   Subjects: Martin, Joan, 1941-2008 — Artists, Aboriginal Australian — Western Australia — Biography Women artists, Aboriginal Australian — Western Australia —Biography.

   Dewey Number: 759.994

Printed in Australia by SOS Print Group

All photographs courtesy Bruce Shaw unless otherwise noted.

Front cover: Detail from Emu Freize, © Joan Martin.

Foreword

A special working relationship developed between Joan Martin, my husband Ron Parker and myself while doing surveys under the *Aboriginal Heritage Act 1972* (Heritage Act). I recall vividly our first encounter, at that time Joan was front page news. A very public figure deeply embroiled in events taking place with Homeswest, and the threatened and subsequent eviction from her home. Australian Interaction Consultants (AIC)* had won a contract to undertake a heritage survey for a proposed service corridor through land subject to the Widi Mob Native Title Claim (NTC). Ron and I approached Joan with some uncertainty due to the media hype surrounding the Homeswest crisis. Joan took a no-nonsense approach as she familiarised herself with the project and made arrangements for Widi representatives to accompany us. Unable to come herself due to the toll of the housing crisis on her health, Joan instructed the people she had carefully selected to make up the survey party.

It was during the first survey with Widi Mob representatives that we became aware that we were working with people who had experienced, first hand, multi-layered trauma: the impact of previous government policies, the dislocation of people, the destruction of heritage and frustration in dealing with Native Title issues. We learned that many Widi people were once engaged in labouring jobs, having gained reliable employment with shire councils, road boards and railways or casual employment with local farmers. Food and rudimentary accommodation were often available with the work and assured that families could stay on their own country. Changes in work patterns and labour conditions, and the associated loss of accommodation, meant many families were often forced to move to urban environments. While Joan was sent away to school, many others were taken to institutions where they had little control over their fate.

By a quirk of fate, a number of subsequent heritage surveys were undertaken in areas of the Midwest subject to the Widi Mob NTC, under the management of Hames Consultancy, the managing director of which was Dr Kim Hames, the former Western Australian (WA) Minister for Aboriginal Affairs and Housing. Whether or not it was to make amends for the hardship caused by his previous involvement in the housing crisis, Dr Kim Hames was instrumental in ensuring that heritage surveys took place with companies that had mining interests in the Midwest. Through him, AIC was engaged for ongoing field trips with Joan and Widi Mob NTC representatives. Kim also took an interest in progressing the NTC through the registration process, to ensure Joan and her family were not left out of negotiating on activities taking place in Widi country.

Over time we became more familiar with Widi country through association with Joan and her mob. We enjoyed the rare privilege of becoming privy to cultural information about country not widely recognised or understood, let alone shared, with whitefellers. A very important aspect of the surveys was the inclusion of her children and grandchildren, to afford them the opportunity to be on their country with their people, and to learn. Joan saw that their future security lay in knowledge of country, understanding legislated processes and knowing their rights.

Work in the heritage arena was far from the trials and challenges of city life, but returning to country brought mixed emotions for Joan. Whilst pleased to be recalling family history with her brother, Bill, and recounting stories to the younger generation, she was often pained by memories of the past. She had a comprehensive knowledge of the history of her people as well as the cultural stories of the land and its features. Attuned to the spirits ever-present in the land from the creative era of the Dreaming, and expressed in the prominent features, she was also disturbed by the potential for mining exploration proposals to progress to full-scale mining and thus the destruction of sites. Her sharp mind and keen intellect, combined with strength of character forged from her experiences, made Joan a force to be reckoned with.

Joan was on the defensive against discrimination and was often forthright and abrasive in her dealings with government departments and mining companies. Born of mistrust from her life experiences, she developed a resilient capacity to provide for and protect all that she loved. Her love and support for her family and her commitment to protecting their cultural heritage was unwavering. She was a true matriarch. It is a cruel twist that when two parties seek to maintain a working relationship where one party stands to gain in economic terms, the

Aboriginal party consulted is ultimately powerless to prevent the interference of, or destruction of sites. Upset by the lack of protection afforded by the Heritage Act, and disillusioned by the role of the WA Department of Indigenous Affairs, Joan was faced with the reality that holding cultural knowledge, whether divulged or not, is insufficient to guarantee protection where the custodian's interest is in the hands of the other. Joan was deeply troubled that she was ultimately powerless to protect significant places subject to mining interests.

Through the surveys Ron became a good friend who provided moral and practical support, assisting Joan during difficult times. He became someone Joan trusted to provide clarification and guidance throughout the process, by interpreting cultural orientations to bridge misunderstandings with agencies and mining companies. There developed between them a relationship characterised by mutual respect and trust. Their association was based upon acceptance, tolerance and genuine interest and concern. I believe they held a unique place in each other's lives through working together, and the understanding that developed over almost a decade essentially made their work possible.

Ron Parker was a great advocate that Aboriginal voices be heard declaring cultural knowledge and authority, and that they be recognised and valued. He did the very best he could to raise the level of understanding about Aboriginal people, their cultural heritage and deep connection to country, and ongoing interest in what happens to the land and its spirits. He encouraged Joan to put her life story to paper and, through AIC, introduced Bruce Shaw to Joan and engaged him for that purpose. In the face of insufficient public awareness and political will, Ron sought to listen beyond the words so as to capture the underlying meaning in all communications. Sadly he passed away. Joan was so deeply grieved that she was unable to attend his funeral.

Through her exceptional artwork, Joan leaves a legacy not only to her family but also to all of us. Joan's paintings, originally compiled as evidence of connection to country to support her claim through the Native Title process, are a body of works representing maps of Widi country and Widi people, and the cultural values embedded in the land. They display her comprehensive knowledge and evoke an insight into her culture. Through them, and through this book, the memories will live on.

Sue Parker
Director & Co-Founder, Australian Interaction Consultants
April 2011

Contents

Foreword		v
Illustrations		x
Preface		xi
Maps		xv–xvi
Genealogical Sketch		xvii
Chapter 1	Reading the genealogies	1
Chapter 2	In the bush	19
Chapter 3	Raising a family	34
Chapter 4	My country	45
Chapter 5	Caring for the land	61
Chapter 6	Dreaming stories	76
Chapter 7	Spirit life	86
Chapter 8	Yarrna	112
Chapter 9	'Since ever the white man came'	131
Appendix	The Homeswest incident	145
Chronology		149
Glossary		158
Bibliography		166
Index		169

Illustrations

Joan Martin	ii
Mabo	117
The half-caste girl	119
The seven sisters	120
The river of life	121
From the guts of the earth	123
Time	123
Hunting kangaroo	124
Hands reaching out	125
Emu and Turkey	126
Wudatjis	127
Bush turkey	128
Beemarra	129
Emus	130

Preface

Joan Martin, a Widi woman, was born as Joan Margaret Lewis in the third year of the Second World War, on 2 March 1941, in the country town of Morawa about 150 kilometres southeast of Geraldton. She passed away around midday on Monday, 6 October 2008. In the words of her eulogy:

> Joan regularly travelled with her family and all who wanted to go bush: to Mount Magnet, Geraldton, Cue, Yalgoo, Mingenew, and Coalseam where her ashes are scattered for the release of her spirit. Joan Martin had many trials and tribulations, many excursions, travels, ups and downs but she always said she would not change a thing. She lived an exciting and adventurous life. Joan's legacy comes from her tireless efforts to protect her family, her cultural heritage, through her art and native title efforts. She pursued these to ensure that her grannies [grandchildren] and children could enjoy and understand their rich cultural heritage. Joan passed away in October 2008. Her life is but a part of the journey of her soul, which began long before her life on Earth. Like her ancestors before her, Ginny of Irwin, Tom Phillips and Jane Phillips, she believed in the spirit of her ancestors, of their country.

Joan's family country centres upon the Morawa area, from Koolanooka and Narandagy to the Dongara coast via the Irwin River. Her great-grandmother (mother's father's mother) was Ginny of Irwin, associated with the Irwin River. Her grandmother Amy Cameron (mother's mother) was the wife of Tom Phillips Junior, a drover who travelled about Widi country and who was a law man of high status. The family storytellers important to Joan were her mother Jane Phillips, Aunt Eva (mother's sister) and Uncle Tom Phillips Junior (mother's brother) born on the Irwin River. Joan's ancestors were the Phillips and the

Cameron families. Her biological father was Norm Harris Senior from the Busselton district. At Joan's request, and with respect, the extensive Harris family is largely omitted from her genealogical chart, because the most important links for her were with her Widi ancestors. Harris family connections are recorded in Lois Tilbrook's groundbreaking set of genealogies *Nyungar tradition* (1983: 118, 122).

Taping Joan's story

Our conversations began on the 12 April 2006. By January 2008 there were twenty-seven 60-minute audiocassette tapes representing about the same number of hours. The work stalled during 2008 due to deaths in Joan's family, her attendance at court hearings to support grandchildren and other relatives in legal proceedings, her successful application for a Homeswest house in Geraldton and subsequent move to that town, and increasing ill-health. Nevertheless, by the time we got back together in August 2008 all but the last two chapters had been proofread.

Twenty-seven hours of recorded time may sound a lot, but the discussions were at Joan's pace and the questioning open-ended, with a minimum of interruptions except to clarify an indistinct word or a misunderstood point. One of the most important research strategies established from 1973, and to which I adhere still, is to take back the manuscript drafts and proofread them line-by-line with the storytellers. My East Kimberley projects (1970s to 1980s) involved reading back the stories to the tellers, crosschecking events, clearing up misunderstandings, and gaining new information. As Joan was a fluent reader, she did the proof-reading herself. At different points in her narrative, Joan was at pains to correct the written record in the genealogies and in the identification of her people the Widi and their traditional country. She supplemented her narrative by drawing upon and critiquing written sources such as Norman Tindale's mapping and Lois Tilbrook's genealogies.

Tapes to manuscript

Oral historians are strong on accurate transcription of the spoken word, by which they mean a faithful word-for-word text incorporating the ellipses, repetitions, digressions and argot representative of the individual's speech community. Adhering too closely to such accuracy for a final draft, however, has pitfalls. David Lodge (1992: 18) states that: 'A narrative style that faithfully imitated actual speech would be virtually unintelligible, as are transcripts of recorded conversations.' He writes from a literary point of view, saying that first-person narration in the mode of the spoken word – *skaz* or street slang – comes from the fiction writer's hard work to create the illusion of spontaneous colloquial speech.

In fact, as most practitioners of oral history know, the utterances they record *are* intelligible although they must edit carefully to avoid the worst moments when a person's narratives become hard to follow. Publishers require this.

Some of Joan's expressions reflect her generation. Such terms were once in common use in her community, whereas nowadays to a younger generation they can be received as disrespectful. For example her use of words such as 'blackfeller,' 'half-caste,' or 'full-blood'. On several occasions, in order to make a point, Joan drew attention to government documents and genealogies where 'fb' (for 'full-blood') and so on appears. She was a very forthright person.

As with other storytellers, Joan repeats information for emphasis, and sometimes circles back to earlier points: 'When I get talking about things I get wrapped in them. Sounds really dramatic. I like pushing a point across' (p. 131). In presenting Joan's speech in type we have tried to maintain her desire for her story to be in 'good English' while allowing her conversational style to shine through.

We have used italics to represent Aboriginal language words (*bungarras*) and have used spellings like *cos* for 'because,' *round* for 'around' and *till* for 'until' to reflect Joan's speech. We have also retained her spellings for people's names and place names.

Words within the text that are included in the Glossary are followed by an asterisk (*) at their first appearance. The Glossary (p. 158–65) provides information about language words that readers might find useful, while the Chronology (p. 149–57) provides a concise summary about Joan's busy life and the historical and family context. Some chapters are longer than others, but they reflect Joan's desire to tell her story in her way. More information is provided in the Appendix (p. 145–8) on the Homeswest incident which was an important event in Joan's life, and to people living in Western Australia, in particular.

This project was carried out during my employment part-time with Australian Interaction Consultants (AIC), whose main business is heritage research between Aboriginal community groups and mining companies or state utilities. Joan Martin asked Ron Parker, AIC head, to help her record her life story. Ron passed on the request to me. I agreed readily and the project commenced on a *pro bono* basis.

The choice of audiocassettes as against digital recording follows best practice at the time as recommended by the Oral History Association of Australia (OHAA) (Robertson 1996: 33–34). Two copies of each audiocassette were made from the original master tapes. They were dubbed on home equipment, a Sanyo GXT 804 Stereo Music System, and transcribed by myself using a Lanier Model VW-110 loaned by the WA Branch of the OHAA, courtesy of Jan McCahon-Marshall (then President of the state branch). Most of the tape recordings were made using a hand-held Sony TCM-359V, also courtesy of the OHAA WA Branch. (Oral historians like to know these things.)

I am indebted to the co-founders of AIC, Sue Parker and the late Ron Parker, the AIC staff, and Joan's two sons Errol Martin and Greg Martin, who read and approved the manuscript. Joan's name and photograph appear at the request of the family. Errors of fact are probably mine. Special thanks go as well to the lively editorial team at Aboriginal Studies Press who brought the manuscript into book form.

Being an oral historian brings one closer to others emotionally, especially over a long period. This is one of the rewards for doing such projects, although it is saddening as well. As we worked together, Joan remarked at one point that she did not wish her story to be told until after she had passed away: 'I don't want it printed until I'm dead and gone' (p. 143).

It was a great privilege to have worked with Joan Martin and to help her tell her story. I have undertaken, as in Joan's words, to put it all in place.

Bruce Shaw
April 2011

Mid-west of Western Australia. Map by Brenda Thornley

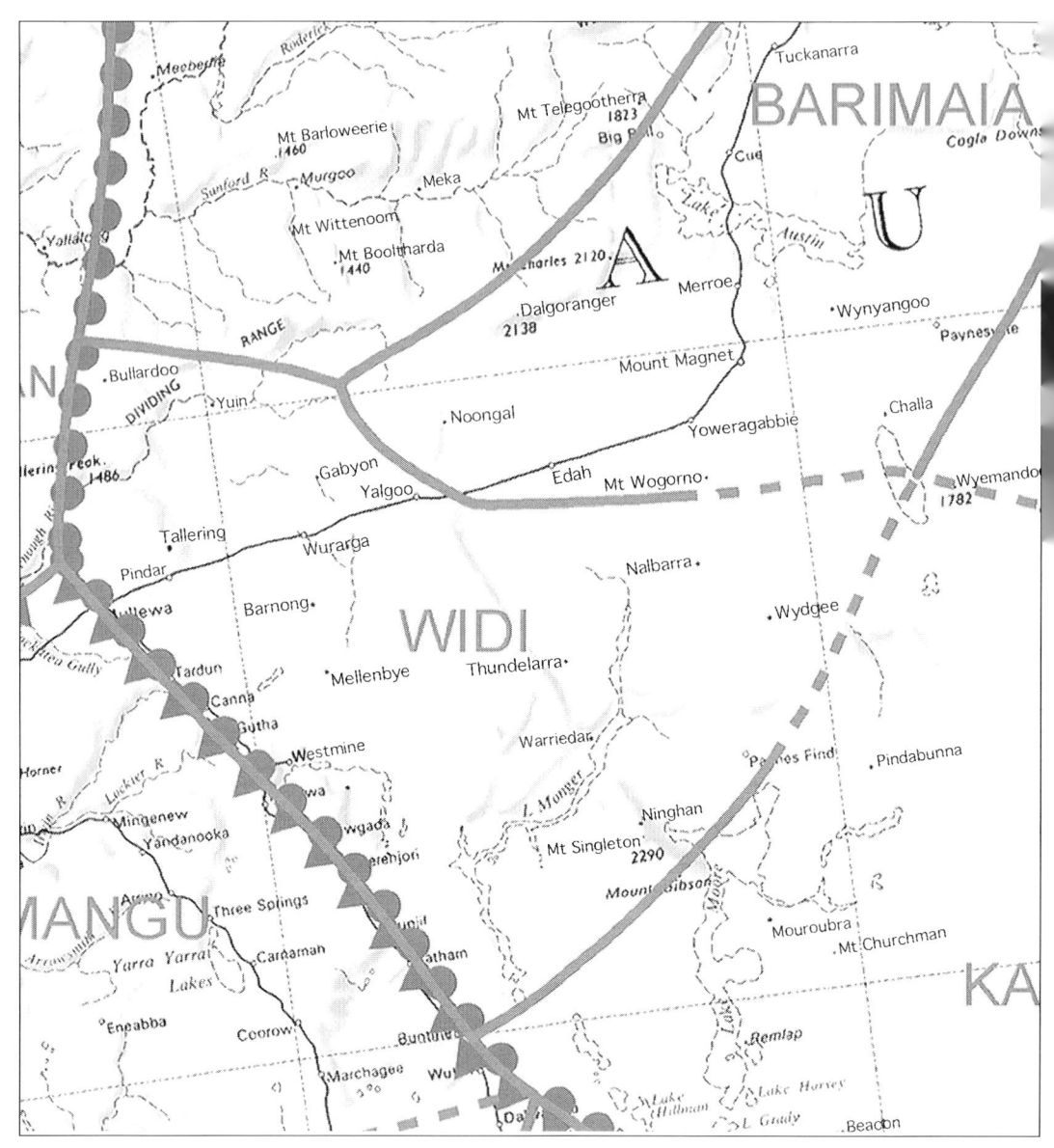

Widi country (Tindale 1974). Courtesy of the South Australian Museum

Genealogical Sketch

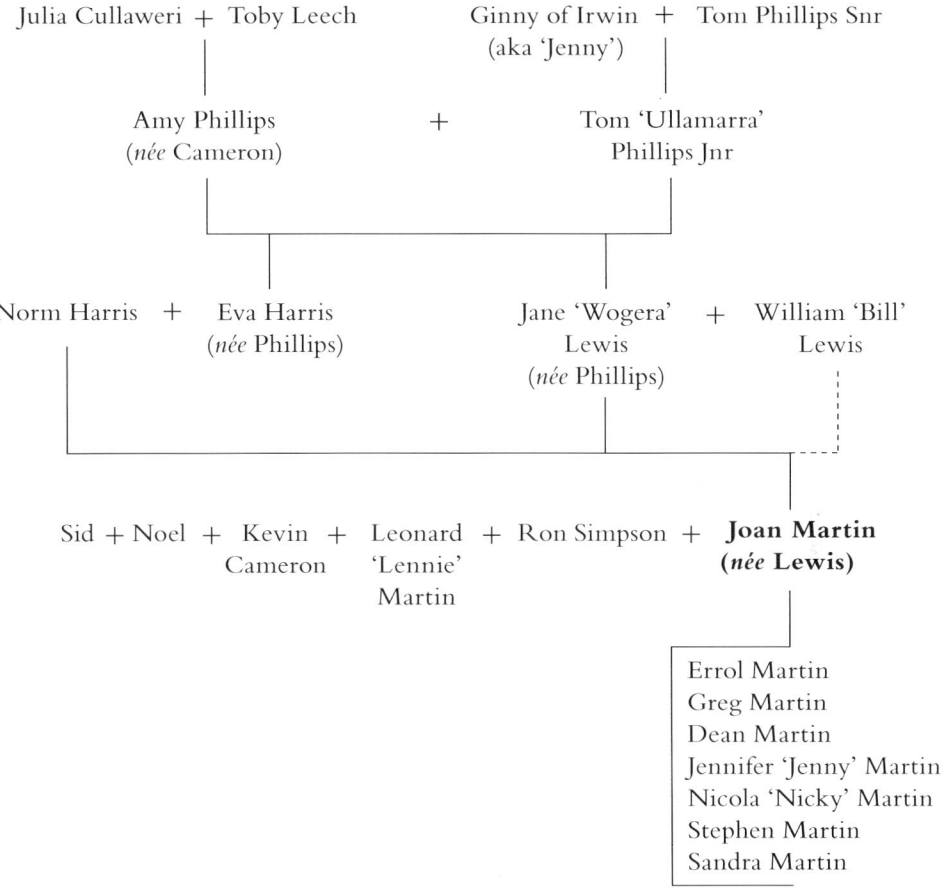

1.
Reading the genealogies

I was born in Morawa* on 2 March 1941 to Jane Margaret Lewis. That's *née* Phillips, but she married Bill Lewis five years before I was born. That's in the Midwest. All except two of our family were born in Morawa. Our camp was down from the pub. It was only a small town.

My family comes from the Midwest and goes back probably to the beginning of time. It comes from Dongara, from the west coast and Jindi up to the boundary in the north, to somewhere further down the coast down south. Anyway it goes east after Dongara, Eneabba down from there to the east, Cue to the north-east, and somewhere near Lake Darlot, and probably close to Coolgardie. All the tribal people from there spoke the same language.

What I'm saying too the way is, my family even though they were born on the Irwin River and came from that area, how would they be able to talk to people as far as Paynes Find if they didn't speak the same language? You know, there's groups of people and that's where they get these skins* from, that they could marry or have partners. But then again they had wife stealing as well.

Widi was made up of different tribes, groups and that's where you get your skin groups, the ones you're allowed to marry and the ones you're not. You certainly weren't allowed to talk: mother-in-laws to son-in-laws and uncles to children, girls in particular. There was no incest in that way. When they went through the law and they were given girls, those girls were from a different skin, men probably of a different group, right across here.

You weren't ever allowed to marry somebody within the tribe. You had skins and that and you could marry different ones from small groups. I don't know my skin name. When my mother was young, I can remember a long way back, she was very afraid of talking about Aboriginal law and her blood parents, because when she went to the Moore River Native Settlement they hoped to stamp out Aboriginal culture and law and forget about the Aboriginal ways.

The Phillips family

The genealogies really start with Ginny of Irwin and Tom Phillips. Whatever her name was I don't know, but that's years before this Charlie Cameron come onto the scene [grandmother's stepfather]. They only came in contact with him because of her son Tom, when he came from there. They lived on the Irwin River.

My Mum's father was known as Tom, and Ginny of Irwin was the great-grandmother [Tom's mother]. She came from the Irwin River. The name Phillips came from one of the white settlers' names. They called them Ginny and Tom Phillips. They were all full-blooded* people and belonged in the Wageral tribe or thereabouts. Only had Ginny and Tom, as far as I know, but this is at the time of white settlement and the people gave them the name. Her name could have been anything. She would have had an Aboriginal name.

I rush when I come here instead of giving the things out properly and get prepared with these genealogies. The genealogies really start with Ginny of Irwin and Tom Phillips, this *maluka**. He was called *maluka*, not Tom Phillips.

These early farmers and settlers that were given land gave him that name Tom Phillips, but they didn't give Ginny another name. She was just Ginny of Irwin. So you know, people when they've got an English name, it's unusual because these are old people born in the 1800s. We estimated Ginny to have been born around the 1850s but we don't know. She came later to be called Jenny instead of Ginny. On the birth certificate of Ginny of Irwin they put Jenny but it was never any more than Ginny. Those people who gave her a name were settlers.

This is the funniest part about it. You know, Jackie and Jenny were typical of the early settlers to call them what they wanted. They said she was about seventy-four when she died on 23 May 1925, so she must have been born around 1851. I'm not aware of her Aboriginal name but the old feller — the old great-grandfather of mine — he was known as *maluka*. His son, young Tom, was Ullamara*. In those genealogies that the government have they've called the old feller Ullamara, but it was young Tom that was that. Something happened to his hand one time. Part of it was sunken in and all his fingers were back. That's why his Aboriginal name was Ullamara — that's referring to his sick hand, *mara** is the hand. When he had to fight the police and that he'd have to close that hand, cos those days, when they were in the missions and things, they had to fight for their rights. So of course they end up in jail. But he was a very strong old bloke and he went to my grandson and said, 'You right.'

My grandfather and great-grandfather were very high in the law there, so they had a great big space all over the place in that area, as people that went around to check on the law ground and the sacred sites, everything like that, and they knew everybody. They'd go from groups of people that belonged to the same tribe, all around in the large area [around Morawa and Widi country in general]. People all spoke the same language.

From the Mount Magnet police station Tommy and John Phillips [mother's brothers] were black trackers some years and years ago. I got their report one time from old Native Welfare days and here I am running around looking for proof of John Phillips being a black tracker, and I remembered — cos my sister's got the same things — she said, 'Oh I saw Uncle John's. He was a black tracker.' 'Oh God,' I said, 'and I've been running around looking for police reports, but it was there all the time!' I just never touched those boxes for a long time. They're up at Errol's now. I've had them the best part of ten years. But you know a lot of information is there, and a lot of information that's unnecessary, a lot of VD [Venereal Disease] talk and sex life of people when what were more important was their journeys. They were only there keeping a count of all the black sheep more or less. That's how you could name it. Cos we weren't voting till '67. We were nobodies. We were branded. All they had was a number name, all my family.

> The death of a stockman. A sudden collapse of Tom Phillips [Senior] near Mingenew. On Sunday morning last an Aboriginal known as Tom Phillips age 70 years died in sudden circumstances on the Depot Hill Road about four miles from Mingenew. Deceased was well known in the district and had the reputation of being an excellent stockman. As a boy he was employed by the late Sam Phillips who at that time resided at the Grange, Irwin and was the owner of most of the land in this district, Mingenew being merely on an out camp of the station.

This came of a research at the Tribunal [National Native Title Tribunal*].

❖

My mother's mother was Amy, and Amy's mother was Julia. Julia Cullaweri. I think it's more like Gullaweri but I saw it spelt as C-u-l-l-a-w-e-r-i. Julia took up with Charlie Cameron after her and her sister were over in Perth and she took that name.

Going back on one side of my mother's family was Julia. That was her grandmother Julia Cullaweri and the daughter being Amy. Then from Amy, when Julia had Amy and Kitty — that was before she was with Charlie Cameron — and Charlie Cameron then fathered Ned, Bill and Fred Cameron, the three men. From there Julia went on and she got with Bill Flannigan, and Bill Flannigan was the father of Bill (William) and Jimmy as we know. But there was also a Bobby Flannigan and Ruby. I'm thinking that they were probably William Flannigan's sister and brother. Because Bobby was a law maker — he carried the law — and him and Amy's father Toby are buried in spiritual belief in the hill east of Morawa, west of Paynes Find, south-west of Yalgoo. It's a big hill there where their spirits are among other people. That was the Widi Mob. The last one to uphold Widi law in that area was Bobby. I don't have any history on him.

Julia's two daughters were Amy and Kitty. Kitty slept with Slavin and Amy with Tom Phillips [Junior]. Amy's father was Toby Leech. Leech or something like that but his name was Toby. I don't know who Kitty's father was, could have been the same. Amy and Kitty could be half-sisters. Then Amy got with Tom, but Julia also got with a William Flannigan, a full-blood Aboriginal. I guess his name was given to him through somebody Irish or something like that. They had children, Bill and Jimmy. So that would be another generation of men. Now there've been other names come up. That was Ruby and Bobby Flannigan. I don't know whether they were Julia's kids or her brother-in-law and sister-in-law.

I don't really know what Kitty went as, Phillips I guess. Very little was known about them only just till recently. Recently I found out that she went with a partner from Mullewa* who came from Kununurra — his name was Jack Simon — and from there they went to work for people, non-Aboriginals down in Collie. They were living at Slavin's Hill. They searched everywhere for her father. Officially they called it Slavin's Hill. I think that's where they lived and died, in Collie, and I don't think any children came out of that marriage. But they didn't come from there. One came from Kununurra and the other one came from Mullewa. That's my grandmother's sister.

I used to listen to my mother's stories — and when she [Amy] ran away from the old feller and was taken to Moore River Settlement she had to be punished because old grandfather was a pretty high person in the law — Amy's husband Tom Phillips Junior. My grandfather was also called Tom Phillips. He used to go away a lot. He had to go and do the rounds of all the sacred sites. They apparently sent this man to take care of Amy because she did run away. She and Mum had a terrible time in Moore River Settlement. He was there to witness (to cause) her death. The man's name was Charlie Chookenau That's what they called him, but Mum called him Charlie Chookener. It's the same man as in these papers.

Well the funniest part about it was when my grandmother died the papers say that she ran away from Tom, the grandfather. She was a bit of a run-around and she left Mullewa with three men. They said her boyfriend was Ned Papertalk. He didn't come from there but they sent him because of Tom being one of the big elders. My Mum told me this. Tom was really a big elder. Well he must have been one of the spokespersons and the main man there. Because she broke that law, he sent one bloke, and his name was Charlie Chookener. Well Mum told me this when I was a kid that he was playing hockey with her in Moore River Settlement and he kept hitting it out to the reeds, the bulrushes. He hit it [the ball] in there and she had to go in there and they waited on her, and they killed her. This old Charlie Chookener was there, but there was a group they call *djinigubbies**. That was their name because *djina* is foot and *gabi* is water.

They were punishing her for running away with that man Ned Papertalk, and they sent Charlie Chookener to kill her, or get her done in as they say. Anyway she only lasted three days after that hockey. Charlie Chookener was one of the tribe. Whether they made him go and punish her or what, but he was there. The story is that he was there. Mum told me.

So when I started this Native Title I had the story on it and of course he's Charlie Chookenau they call it in the [Native Welfare Department file], the white man's spelling. His name was on it to help the grandfather Tom bury his mother, Ginny of Irwin. So he's still within that tribe when Amy the daughter-in-law died in Moore River Settlement. But when they took her, the Welfare and that, she was pregnant and it was only just after that baby was born that they killed her. They let the baby be born with my Uncle Frank. But then they took the villain, Ned Papertalk, and they pushed him through the law for twelve months punishment. He didn't really come from there. He came from Wadjari people and they killed him anyway in the end.

The reason they called them 'papertalks'* is because he had no name and he was delivering the mail up in the station out of Mullewa. He was a mailman and I guess all these neddies (horses and things) they gave them their name papertalk, because he was bringing the mail, the 'paper talk'. That's how that name came. Well you're reading paper. The white people did it. He'd ride with that mail and he was bringing the paper talk, letters and things. They'd say, 'Oh papertalk coming,' I suppose. It wasn't our word really.

That was strange. My mother told me this story about Charlie Chookener more than fifty years ago. I must have been only six when I knew the story, so it would have been sixty years ago she told me the story. Then blow me down, when Native Title started — that's ten years ago — I looked in the papers and his name is on the death certificate of her grandmother Ginny of Irwin.

My uncle told me lots of things in a roundabout way, and my aunty. They were going to kill her when she was born because she was fairer and perhaps not Tom Phillips's daughter. So they were going to kill her as a baby and this other old lady, Fanny Comeagain, saved her and took her and reared her up and she lived in Mullewa. Comeagain's another invention for names, 'come again'. Well they were all Biddies and Ginnies and Marys and Jackies weren't they? I mean that was common. But they had an Aboriginal name.

Jane Margaret Phillips

I was thinking that I didn't even mention my mother, what sort of person she was. A very strong person she was. She was a big strong woman. My mother's background is from the Wageral tribe. They're on the Irwin River. Some of it's pronounced differently because it's an Aboriginal name, and it's hard to put that proper spelling into those names. But all the ancestors, that was their area. My mother's name was Jane, and her nickname was Wogera*, her Aboriginal name of that Wageral tribe.

1. Reading the genealogies

I never knew those names were necessary until Native Title came up. I think she was given the name when she was born because they were born in tribal first, covered in ashes, ash powder like talcum powder and born there on the river. The only one born in the hospital was Frank. They were all tribal people reared up to speak the language, eat the food and obey the law. There was no other.

Eva was the eldest. The next was Horace, Jane third, then John, Tom, Reg and Frank. Reg died when he was about ten or eleven years. They lived with us. More like a cousin, Tom's [mother's brother] daughter Irene. I don't think it's a cousin. It's a strange thing. You can pick it up through the history, Welfare work. I'm not sure whether she's a full-sister. There's a question mark about Irene, because it mentions that Tom's daughter Irene could have been a mistake.

My mother was a full-blood and she was born on the banks of the Irwin River, about ten kilometres south of Mullewa and west of Gutha Siding. In the history done by the old Native Welfare she was born in Mullewa, but it wasn't, it was on the river as were her brothers and sister, except one and that was Frank. He was born in Moore River Settlement. My mother was taken away to that settlement when she was twelve with her mother and brothers. She was quite big and strong in her young days, but I don't think she was any more than five foot six [167 cm]. They had no names and were just known by different places. They would have had Aboriginal names, but those names went with the passing of the elders.

At that time you see my mother wasn't allowed to talk about the law and culture, only the old feller when he came, Tom Phillips Junior. He used to come every now and then. He used to go round and round and that. This was at Karara Station where we're doing a lot of site clearances. He had work there, and my mother worked there too as a housemaid, but only during the holidays from Moore River Settlement. But he got mixed up with one of the old people there and there was a daughter. Her name was Gladys. She was younger than Mum I think. Gladys got married. She married a *wajela** [white man]. Kennedy, Gladys Kennedy. Her children are like my first cousins because it's Mum's sister. But that's where he picked up with Ada. Her mother's name was Ada Mudigu and she was living in blackfeller* way married to old Albert Kennedy. Old Ada had different families. They were Widi people as well.

My old Dad he was an old whitefeller* you know and he was going out to work in the farm. He got a shilling off the boss to just go and have a drink before he went and the police ran across. He said, 'I'll have you Bill.' 'What for?' 'Begging alms.' But it was funny because the blooming farmer was a JP [Justice of the Peace] as well. He said, 'He'll never go to jail for it, I can tell you now, cos he's working for me, and if I choose to give him money he can have it.'

My biological father was old Norm Harris, quite big build too. There are a lot of Norm Harrises I might add. The man who was my father was born from Annie and Arthur. They were both Harrises. They were first cousins I believe. They ran from the sou-west up there to get away from their family because it was an inbred sort of thing. Whoever would think that the first cousins would want to get married? But they do. When they adopt these kids you have sister and brother marrying as well. There's no limit to what can happen.

Only two names have been passed down. That's my father Norm and his son Norm. The son called Norm is my cousin. My father Norm had two wives, my mother and her sister. Eva was the eldest sister. My Aunty Eva shared her husband with my mother to produce children. Norm Junior comes from my mother's sister. Not only is he my first cousin, he's my brother. Norm Harris was my mother's sister's husband but he was also my father. He shared the two sisters. It was like so many other things you know. Aboriginal people are used to doing that. At his funeral there were all these people and old old whitefellers that had been there all their lives. It was the respect he gained through the years, my biological father Norm Harris. They've got a park up in Morawa they call Harris Park. They knew we come from there.

My stepfather was Bill Lewis, a white man. He reared us up as his own. He couldn't have children, the old whitefeller, but he was happy with what happened. Only we weren't happy, see, when we found out. Aboriginal people do it over Western Australia and all over, that agreement that the brother or the sister should take over in case of death or sickness, and it's normal. Only we didn't know about it.

Aboriginal people, look you never find somebody that's virgin, doesn't matter how hard you try. In the old days I'm talking about. They've always been second hand and have always got children. They always had that policy of when your partner dies, if it was a woman, the brother takes over or a sister takes over. That was a reasonable law I'd say. The main thing is you see, let the sister look after them because that's the closest thing to me you know, and that's it, that's what happened with her.

There were three Harrises in our family. They were actually my half-sisters and brother. I had the same father and different mother and there were always people called them our cousins. It didn't matter to me because they were my cousins till I found out the truth. The old people never told you the truth until you were grown up. That's why a lot of these genealogies and things, you couldn't bet a million bucks on them because they're unreliable, and if you don't know your background from the time you can talk you're lost, cos you can claim anybody for your father. When you register kids, even today, you can tell them, 'oh, father unknown'. So when that happens they put 'father unknown'. It makes a real bad person out of you, but people don't always want to tell everybody who's the father of their children. It works well in one way, but in another way there's always those chances of inbreeding and that sort of thing.

I think it was a built-in shame* from the times of white settlement and the Moore River Settlement. People didn't talk about it. When they did talk about half-brothers and half-sisters, well it was some time later you know, because my mother and her sister very rarely spoke of them. I didn't know until I was twenty. Norm Harris was an Aboriginal from Busselton but he had a white background, that Jane Bussell. They were direct descendants of Jane Bussell. I've got those clippings that Jane Bussell saved people from drowning.

I have one half-brother died in 2005. The kids were never taught that my family was related to them closer than they thought. They thought, 'Oh that's Mum's cousin,' Mum or Dad's cousin. I never ever respected that because they were taught, 'No that's shame.'

But the man that we know as father was a white man who met my mother in Morawa or Mingenew. At that time they had a compound and he wasn't allowed inside that compound and they had to camp outside. That was in Mingenew where they put Aboriginal people, where they were allowed to camp. More like a reserve now but they called it a compound in those days. That's what Mum described it as. They had a camp outside the compound. But I think that compound — they said Mingenew — related to more when she went out to the Coalseam and they camped out there.

This is history they've collected at the Tribunal. Their research is quite out. 'William George Lewis' — that's my stepfather — 'died on the 23rd of August aged 77. He was later buried at Karrakatta Cemetery in Perth ... in the lawn section.' That's ridiculous. That's unbelievable to say he was buried at Karrakatta Cemetery; he was buried in Mount Magnet. Well my son was about four, and he would have been forty-six this year. He's been gone forty-two years my old Dad, the white man that reared us up, and they reckon he was seventy-seven. It's so confusing. They've got heaps of different names. But they didn't confuse me because I just followed what my mother said, and what she knows, and what she told me.

The Harrises and the Camerons

They were pioneers his father, in the Morawa district. They had quite a big family and they settled on farmland out of Morawa. This is my real father, Norm Harris. They were originally from Busselton and they came with their people. Anyway they cut everything down, made a farm out of it, and the old man died. But that was land given. He was treated like a prisoner. You know like how they gave him land to work at no costs, then when he died it was a good piece of land and prosperous and so they said, 'Oh no he never paid his tax.' So they took it back.

He was a real hard-working old feller. I can barely remember him. I saw photos of him and his brothers and they were very straight-backed, soldier-like in appearance, and well dressed, as well as any white man of the day, hat and coat and collared shirt and things like that, very straight-laced. That was Norm Harris in that delegation. My kids are well aware of who they are. I don't believe in hiding cos when I die they can say what they like about me. The old clan was very strict. We weren't told and we weren't to know, that's for sure. The elders' business you know. But underneath it all they really cared for us and that's the way. I mean they taught us things. He came from down here and they said his family was very strict, old Norm. He was one of the first blokes that went in as a delegate to the government over land rights years ago [1928], Norm Harris, old, old fellers.

Charlie Cameron was only a name. You know how Aboriginal people, when the wives get remarried they claim the children and give them a name. Really we're not Camerons. My grandmother had brothers that were Camerons, like Julia after. When she got with Charlie Cameron she already had Kitty and Amy. Then she went with Charlie Cameron and she had three Camerons. That was Ned, Fred and Joe.

1. Reading the genealogies

Norm Harris gave the description of his ancestors as Camerons and Harrises. See there's lots of things written in my cousin–brothers' history that he gave to the Battye Library and you can get papers, like it's a conversation. Norm Harris's. Cousin-brothers are first cousins, the mother's brother's children or the mother's sister's children. A couple of things he wrote were wrong. Like he believed — and I tell you that only the last ten years or so we found out that the grandmother [Amy] wasn't a Cameron at all. But, if I were to listen to the older feller [Norm Harris] when I was eighteen it all came out then. She was somebody's child but she wasn't a Cameron. They told us the name of some other feller, a first name, Toby Leech or something like that. He's buried out in our country there. Well he would have been a great-grandfather or grandfather to me. He was the father of Amy, so great-grandfather. Amy was not a Cameron. But there was a lot of that in Aboriginal history. She might have taken the name of Cameron because her mother lived with a Cameron and she had three children after.

One old feller — old Leedham Cameron — told me when I was about eighteen, 'Oh, where's old girl now old sister? My big niece? Well not my niece really,' he said, 'but we claim her.' I thought it was strange all through my life because they never claimed anyone else in that family.

Ned Cameron is the man that taught me how to cook a scrambled emu egg without a pan and baking it Aboriginal way. They're old Jack's sisters and I can't remember what name they told me. See this woman that wrote these pieces up Ruth Fink, was there in '56. That's how old they are. She also recorded songs from Mullewa and he was the main one used to sing. There's quite a few songs. She brought them over and she called a meeting and I went up there for it, I think in January. I was pretty crook but I wasn't going to miss it so I signed myself out of hospital.

In 1946 Charlie Cameron died, so you could question whether he was as old as Ginny of Irwin or Julia. But our life's history doesn't start with Charlie Cameron. Ours comes from Ginny. When Charlie Cameron died in 1946, well they were long gone thirty or forty years before.

Narandagy and Mingenew

There's a hill they call the Mingenew Hill but it's actually a sacred site, a Dreaming* site that's for ants. My mother called ants *minga-minga** but other people have just called it *minga*. When you look at the name 'Mingenew' and see how close that hill is to the town, Mingenew, it's named after the ants. *Minga,* ant. I'll bet anything you like the name comes from that Ant Dreaming and *minga,* the Aboriginal name. Ants eat porcupine* and mountain devil. I was never told about the Ant Dreaming but I know it was there. You find two little black ants with a red stripe across their back. They're sacred. They're the feeders. They track those little things and they take them back underground.

Coalseam is quite a few miles out, about thirty-three kilometres. My cousin Norm Harris went to stay with them [family] most holidays and weekends from Yandanooka near Mingenew. When they were out there, it was more or less an Aboriginal settlement of people, groups, cos it was somewhere there at Narandagy that my great-grandmother Ginny of Irwin was buried. There were camps there on the way to the Coalseam. Narandagy is in between the Coalseam and Mingenew. Anyway she was buried there, and they had big camps there. When my mother was small her grandmother, Ginny of Irwin, towards her later years couldn't walk. She had a back problem.

I read a little piece in Mingenew in the pub that spoke about a big Aboriginal man, tall, curly hair and he used to dress up at certain times. His name was Phillips. He must have been my great-grandfather.

They lived there. That was their settlement all their lives until they died and they buried Ginny at Narandagy. Of course they had to take her away from the river to bury her. I know how to find them. I came back and had a look at her death certificate, got it through the Welfare. It says she was buried at a hundred metres in from Narandagy. That's not far but there are farms everywhere. There's just one little part, a bit of bush. It's not only culturally significant, it's fascinating. It's scary, brings my mother closer to me. I did not live at Narandagy. I reckon I'd be too scared. I've been through Mullewa, around it, not Narandagy. I was really pleased to see the directions there on that road. But I didn't know that trail was in a hundred metres from Narandagy.

We can look through the bush for the grave. They mark it with trees. They square it off. Well the trees die. We found one the other day and the archaeologist told us it wasn't. It's annoying. Like I said you know, you wait for a white man to confirm whether you're telling the truth or not. They're spread around in a square then marked like that. They lay dead trees round, whatever square. I've never taken much notice. They're round the edge of it. In other places when there's no soft ground they put them in the crevices in the hills, and chock-a-block that crevice with wood and stones so animals don't get to them. I don't know if they're sticking up or not but they're in the rocks in between. We're not to know. That's what they do. They don't talk about those things. That's the last thing on your mind.

I keep thinking about how they must have lived. There was nothing. I mean, when I visited that area it was so plain to see why they called it *widi*. In the languages surrounding like, Wadjari people called it *widi* which is meant to be 'no good' or 'savage'. The country is savage. When you drive out of Mingenew towards the Coalseam you think you're on level country, but when you get out there the hills are just cut away and you're looking down into valleys, valleys from everywhere. The Irwin River itself in its time when it had plenty of water must have been a really deep, deep river. See, the sides of the river are just cut away. Just think how they lived. They had no clothes then. Their bodies must have been hardened to it. They had kangaroo skins I guess if they were lucky, but most of them walked naked there. My mother told me. They used to have a little rag on. I don't know what it was made of but probably kangaroo skin. But it's so wild it's just unbelievable, and so unexplored. You could spend twelve months, two years, a hundred years and you'd never know the secrets because there's so much there to look at.

My mother was born there along the Coalseam. I don't want them [the mining companies] to go across that certain part, and there's a lot more sites that should be seen and registered. Like they let them go out in the time, you know when the files were first registered with the old Native Welfare Department, and then if you don't revive that they're gone forever.

That Coalseam, Ron Parker wanted to come with us on a survey. Cos at Mingenew they reckon it's the land of many rivers. But if you only saw it, it's so scary in one way and it's not in another you know, but you think about how that water must have rushed in, in the time. These ravines, if you went too far up the top of the hill you'd drop down onto the plain. Anyway, that's something you wonder what happened there for those people to inhabit the land. Ron said to me, 'It's not hard to imagine, Joan. They've got the food, they've got the water, they've got everything, hiding places.' CALM* [WA Department of Conservation and Land Management] wants to make it a tourist place to look over the Irwin Valley. But if they really want them up there I don't. And if it's a money-making venture well all the more reason why they shouldn't. We wouldn't sell our country.

The tribal people of Narandagy were called Wageral*. The tribal name was Wageral. Just imagine names that made up the Widi and they were camped in different areas along the river. The river is the main thing. It's a Dreaming line. Actually, when my mother was born they called her Wogera which meant somewhere where she was born by the river.

There were quite a few families around Narandagy, different little groups. I know Comeagains and Flannigans were there. Flannigans came out to be quite a big family cos old Uncle William Flannigan — I'm talking about three or four generations back Flannigans he had the same mother as Amy, my grandmother. Eva Harris can be put on that list. Eva Harris lived with Comeagains in Mullewa. *Née* Phillips. She was Eva Phillips before and Cameron was her name, her line.

My aunty must have been fathered by somebody else but known as Eva Phillips. She was a lot fairer than my mother. My mother was a full-blood and it was a shame for us because it was known that we were fathered by my uncle, besides it being Mum's sister you know. But they never failed in caring for us. Both Eva and Norm cared for us. They'd check us out for everything. They'd make sure we were fed. They'd come regularly and see my Mum and Dad and they'd make sure we didn't have sores or sore eyes or anything.

Those other families have an interest because it was settled there you know, farming country. They killed a hell of a lot of people out. They chased them inland and that's a long time ago those people. A lot of them are dead, Tom, John and Frank, Horace, Jane Lewis and Eva Harris.

I went up to my uncle's funeral in Carnarvon. That was my Uncle Horace Phillips. When we hit the corner — they were all on this block, they called it Kelly's Block — I could hear all the old boy's in-laws shouting. We came round the corner and we saw people running with a big canvas sheet and they put it on the ground. They put a blanket over the top of that and the minute we pulled up they came and they led us to sit in that circle on that thing. Oh there were people after people after people, and I didn't know quite when to come in.

Departmental records

These [records] came from Family and Children's Services, but they work in conjunction with the Aboriginal Affairs. It's not far from the Aboriginal Medical Service in Silver City. See a lot of these letters were written because Tom Phillips [Junior] the grandfather couldn't read and

1. Reading the genealogies

write. This here was written by Eva's husband, Norm Harris. That's his writing. There's a lot of interesting things in it, interesting and yet sad, and personal and all that sort of thing you know, how they talked about your forefathers being this and that. A lot of the letters go on about diseases and things. A sad case because they didn't have any choice of telling him. They were treated like the American Negroes, slaves you know.

That's why I say a lot of it's mixed up, not quite what they think, but it's all there. They're not really absolutely correct. It's what they wanted to hear and say themselves. But of course the Chief Protector he was the boss of all the blackfellers and we only had numbers didn't we until 1967, then we were recognised as being human.

This is when my mother got her citizenship rights. This one is Willie Lewis of Morawa: 'Little more than a quadroon.' See: 'Mr Lewis was a half-caste but there was sufficient evidence on the other files to indicate that he has a greater preponderance of native blood, and is really of very dark skin. I am satisfied that he is more than a quadroon.' All these, three-quarter caste, half-caste* and oh gee whiz. They really didn't have any idea because the white man [Bill Lewis] wasn't our father and they're talking about skin things and that. Quite funny.

I think this is my mother's. Well that one is actually Tom Phillips's history. That's the father of Janey. This is when we were more or less going to be taken away, and we could have been part of the Stolen Generation. But they gave her the option of getting out of the camp where we lived in Morawa and that's it all there. They called my old Dad a waster, poor old feller: 'Drunken waster whose desire is to take the boy from school and send him to work,' 1 December 1946. See they're watching us all the time: 'So that his progress may be watched.' 'He has secured his Junior Certificate and may be possible to bring this boy to Perth so he has further education.'

Well he did that. They did exactly that, the three eldest ones. This all came about. That was really bad and it left me like I didn't know where I was. I didn't know there were any other Aboriginals in the world, just our two families. I had no idea. We did have visitors but they were very few and far between. As for living in tribal things, I couldn't say that I didn't know, cos I did. My Mum took me to funerals in Mullewa. An old lady by the name of Marjorie Pearce died and I remember distinctly going to that funeral with my mother. She had to put us on the goods train. We got on the goods train and away we went to Mullewa. Mum had to go to all those funerals of the people in Mullewa.

Amy ran away, and Wunnara Station is one of the places where she lived and worked, way over there near Paynes Find as well. They were working for money that they never saw. They didn't see it because it was kept by the government. The government had just come around in '75. Seven and sixpence [75 cents], well the government gave fifty cents. But even the two and sixpence [25 cents] they never saw. Wunnara Station, they lived there. It was part of their lifestyle. A lot of places they sent them to. There's one here in particular up near Mount Magnet, Mullin Station where the station owner wrote to the Chief Protector and asked him whether he could get Tom Phillips to do some droving, and he said he was a good man.

The Moore River Settlement

My grandmother [Amy] was taken from Mullewa where she was caught by the police and sent to Moore Rover Settlement with the kids, not so long before Frank was born, somewhere in the early 1920s. Mum was about eleven or twelve, but she never went to school until they went into the settlement. Then she learnt to speak fairly well, good English. But she kept a lot of Aboriginal language, her and her sister.

My mother must have had a totem because she went through the law. There was a lot of initiation to do with that and the tools that they used. Of course they were taught who they were not allowed to talk to, who they weren't allowed to marry, and what their business was in life, all those things. Respect was one of the big orders. You had to respect those people. But she wasn't allowed to talk [in lingo*]. That was the white man's rules we had to live with, because Norm and his family when they were educated they were settled there. They were like Australians who'd been reared up like white people.

See my mother — the two sisters — weren't allowed to talk [in lingo] because Norm Harris didn't know their lingo. He'd been the leader of the gang. He didn't like the two sisters talking, 'Take your bloody tribal language.' (They would never swear actually.) I never read into any of these history and things, mainly because we weren't reared up there at Morawa.

I think that's one of the worst things that they ever did for us you know. They took away our culture. That's Moore River Settlement. My mother used to run away continually. They fed her bread and water, and when they let her out she'd do it again. It was also in her history but she told me about it.

They did a very good job I'd say when they pushed them all into Moore River Settlement. A really good job because those people are lost. They don't know where they come from. You can't blame the people for claiming the land where different ones are, because that's all they can do is to claim, 'I come from there, I was born there.' But their ancestors don't, and the ancestors didn't tell them anything.

They mention the children being sent to Sister Kate's from the Moore River Native Settlement. The only one that went there was my mother and her brothers. Sister Kate's was for white, fair kids. That's where they hoped to outbreed the blacks, and the only ones that went there were the fair ones. All the black ones had to go to the settlement.

They put the black ones out on stations to work for station owners who in turn had big parties where they invited all the menfolk to use the black girls. The brother of one of them — I met her in Melbourne — she got out of Western Australia cos she couldn't handle it after. She was young when she and her brother were put on a station, she told me. Actually it was a woman's conference they held in Melbourne in 1993 it must have been. I went to it and she put her testimony in. But the testimony was read out by somebody else because she was still under that pressure. She's a bit older than me. They put them out and asked all the farmers around the district to come for a party. The brother was younger than her. He could hear her screaming and screaming and screaming while they raped her in bed, abused her. This was out from Moore River Settlement, one of those stations. They just placed them. It didn't matter what farm, but that's what the government was doing to them, used them as sex tools. Terrible things happened to them.

They tried that with my mother. But she was a very stubborn person (I suppose I take after somebody) and she used to run away and try to get back to Mullewa. She'd run away to Mogumber and Walebing, all those stations you see along there, and they'd catch her and take her back. They'd put her in the clink they called it, in the boob*, and feed her on dry bread and water. Sometimes she'd be in there for weeks. Well it made her all the more stubborn and she'd do it again. She used to go with a group of people.

I can see now how my mother lived. It was terrible — well to me and to people like yourself and that — that's why they took them away, supposed to be for the betterment of Aboriginal people. But they were doing fine in the bush. I mean, when we were up there in the Coalseam the anthropologist said, 'Why would they want to move from here? They got fish in the river. They got food, they got everything they want there in that Coalseam.'

When my mother came out of the mission they tried to stop her from going back to culture and things. But when she left there she went through the Aboriginal law. There was no law in this coastal region that the Amangu* claimed to be theirs. Well Amangu is just an Aboriginal name for 'my sole informant' and they didn't do the law there. There was no circumcision. It was part of Widi actually. They had to go east of Mingenew and Dongara to go through that law. Well my mother had to go up to Mullewa way. It's only a stone's throw. That's the circumcision line. It does say in Tindale's thing that it was Amangu of Widi. They were Widi people because they had the one law. People go on and say, you know, 'Oh that's Amangu law.' But there was no such thing as Amangu law.

2.
In the bush

We had an old camp just in the bush near Morawa and Koolanooka. We had a dirt floor that during the summer Mum would dampen down with water and stop the dust from rising, just sprinkle this water on. She only had an old bush broom made from this shrub, and if you got caught on a splinter from that shrub, oh God it pained. I don't know what sort of bush it was but it was our bush broom. Anyway it did the trick, used to keep the yard clean and the camp clean.

Did I ever tell you how we had to live as children, bits and pieces, our first bed? My Mum used to chop this gum tree down till she got a fork of a tree. So they put that down, four corners, and she'd go to the dump or wherever, pick up some wire and stretch it across, across and across. Then she'd look for the finest of trees. There's a soft bush up there. That was our mattress. Wheat bags over to cover that and canvas, often from the CBH [Cooperative Bulk Handling Limited], was our blanket. So anybody who's been to a mission was far out better off than us.

We were happy. That's the part that's missing in these stories. Every morning I'd wake up and greet the day and think I was lucky to be alive. I was happy with myself and my family, happy to be alive and where I was. Didn't matter that we had nothing. It didn't matter at all you know. What we had we were satisfied with and we were really healthy.

Ants used to bite the heck out of us, bull ants. Meat ants we used to call them. Oh we knew all about it if we walked on one of them. There were bunches of ants. Couldn't have meat. They'd raid us. They were like pirates.

Neither did any of us get snake-bitten and the snakes were everywhere. Mum used to call them 'Joe Blake'*. We had a bush shed — a bough shed* — and at night you could hear them going through the bottom of that and they'd make this noise, shhhhhhh ... shssssss, just quietly. She'd say, 'Oh, old Joe Blake's here now.' This was daily and nightly. It wasn't just one-off that we saw them. Those snakes we sort of accepted and the old feller [Joan's stepfather] used to get up and kill them or do what he had to. It was not a problem. We grew up with snakes and spiders and all those things. Now I see people freaking out, 'This is a snake!' or a spider. I can't believe it.

We loved life, the whole lot of us. We got our thrills out of playing with things. Maybe if we were lucky we'd wheel a tyre back from the dump and when the winter came we'd slide around with that tyre. My brother used to put us younger ones, my sister Shirley and myself, in the tyre and wheel it across the flat. Of course when it stopped it fell in the mud and we were more times caked in mud than anything else, but we'd slide around in it. It was just fun. We had that happiness with us. The other things I got must have been spiritually you know, contact with the old people. I knew what I had to eat. We lived off the land. We never had money. They told me afterwards it was Depression times.

I used to wander through the bush every morning during the winter fascinated by the big spider webs. They were everywhere. I was careful not to knock or break them. The only reason I broke a small one would be to get through. The art of that spider web was something that fascinated me no end. I had to go and check it every day, early in the morning when the dew was on it and it was like drops of jewels. Cos the little drops of dew in the morning sun was like diamonds. You know they'd give out all different colours. I never got over them anyway. There were hundreds of them, big spiders, big grey things with stripes across their legs. I guess it's those things they call tarantulas but we had no fear for them. There was no fear. I just didn't want to break their web cos they were made so carefully, and to me it was a work of art and beauty.

We used to torment the trapdoor spider. When you chased it, it kept down, and while we're pulling the trapdoor — you could get hold of that — he was pulling from the other side and it's pretty hard to open that trapdoor. We used to have fun. They never used to bite us or anything. We never had that kind of problem.

Living off the bush

During that time before going to Perth we lived on the best we could, on Aboriginal food and water. My mother and uncle and aunty taught us lots of things about the bush, about animals, birds, what to eat, what not

2. In the bush

to eat, seeds off trees, porcupines [echidnas], and all those sort of things. I think probably our main diet was porcupines. It was easier for us to catch a porcupine than it was to catch an emu. We didn't have guns. We tracked the porcupine until they'd run into a hollow log.

When they'd come in from the bush Eva and Norm Harris would bring us food in the way of an emu or a kangaroo. But before that I don't know what. I remember eating birds and *bungarras**. Mum would have to catch them, and some of the white people around there offered a rabbit trap so we were lucky enough to get a rabbit. I don't know that rabbits belong here but this was in the early days. My Mum reckoned they used to eat bobtails* up in Onslow and in Mingenew. I wouldn't eat them, but she ate them on the coast there. Her home ground was near Dongara, all along that river, and there are bobtails there rather than *bungarras*, and that was her meat. It's a coastal land fish, the bobtail. All along the coast they still eat them, bobtails instead of *bungarras*. They call them perentie in the whitefeller's ways, racehorse goanna. But we had different kinds of *bungarras*. We had black ones. The black ones we weren't allowed to eat. They were the law makers to us. But there was a diamond headed one around Morawa when I was a kid. Pretty things. But I didn't like them either because they've got a snow white fat, rather than the yellow fat on the *bungarras* that they usually eat. I was taught how to survive in the bush. The kurrajong tree was a source of water. I knew there was fresh water could be found in creeks. We had to dig for it.

I just had a one-track mind on what I was reared up on, porcupine, emu eggs, and those other birds they call *nyiawl**. They lay these pretty little pink eggs in a big mound, mallee hens. My aunty used to dig them out like with a fine-tooth comb, very gently because the shell was very delicate. You know, you'd put your finger through the eggs. Mallee hen eggs are paper-thin and they're pink, a pretty pink. And you have to be very, very careful when you dig for them. You can't go along with a shovel and dig. That's not on. She'd bring them home. That was a luxury. We didn't have fowls and if it was eggs, well it was either emu eggs or mallee hens.

Also, I watched the old people spinning an emu egg — we call it spinning now — in order to have a scrambled egg. They'd put a hole in the top of one egg, and a long stick from a tree, a twig in and they'd stir it all up. Break the yolk, stir it up and they'd turn it upside down to seal that little bit. They'd put it in the hot sand to seal that opening while they puncture the other end, and they'd do the same thing there. While it's in the hot ashes they'd rub them, only sort of spin it, so all the time that it was in the hot ashes it was cooking. They were spinning it and it was going round and round, and they'd stop and they'd turn it upside down and they'd wipe away so much sand you know, but all the time it was cooking down the end, and they'd stir it up again. They'd stir it up until the egg actually stood up and it was heavy. Then they'd break it open and just eat what they wanted. It was something like hard-boiled but it was all scrambled.

I was really fascinated because, I thought, 'How would they do that?' They said, 'Oh, we eat the egg.' Sometimes they'd crack them with a stone and put them in hot ashes, so long as they just cracked them and they didn't bust and go everywhere. They cracked the egg before they put it in the hot ashes and straight away that crack would seal but the egg would cook anyway. They wouldn't have had anything to cook them in, so nine times out of ten they'd be cooking them in the ashes.

But cooking kangaroo tails or kangaroos in the ashes, it's not really the ashes that they cook it in. It's the sand, heated by putting small amounts in the fire and heating until it was very hot. This is the Aboriginal's traditional way of cooking kangaroos. They warmed the stones in the fire and they kept on shovelling sand from the creek into it, creek sand. What they actually did was heated the sand up to cook this kangaroo in the heated sand, the kangaroos and the tails. The stones would go into the stomach. I don't think that mob had anything to do with salt. I know the Wongis* weren't allowed to eat salt. It was an insult. The finer parts of that kangaroo would go to the men. They had everything, all the delicacies or whatever they considered. I know one feller wouldn't eat anything but the kangaroo head. His wife had to cook it up. That's one of Irene's husbands.

We used to go out every winter when the emus started laying eggs. They used to track them for miles. The emu was running in a circle, and sometimes rushing a fox, sometimes rushing something. You could see the tracks and all the skids. He'd rush out and that could be round and round in a circle, a hundred yards [91.4 m] or something. I was young when I saw it. Then you'd see these little toenails. That's all they could walk on when they go into that nest, clip-clip. I had some fun trying to chase one off their nest — wanted those eggs. See, those fellers, they eat them with chicks in them. It's like a delicacy. Boil them up and they pick the bones and things. I don't. But we took the eggs and ate them all. There were two chased us. I believe it was a male. He chased us and chased us till he couldn't chase us any longer. We took the eight eggs. There were hundreds of eggs in the bush.

It'll be a good year to see a cyclone kick it right off. Then they'll be laying like mad. Then you look in the sky you'll see an emu in the Milky Way. If our Emu is pointing down, it's laying. If it's up in the air, well she isn't quite laying but she's getting ready to lay the eggs. Ever seen those ones before they're sort of ready to come out, pretty and coloured? Pretty, pretty. But the ones before they're ready, they're only small you know but they are a beautiful milky green. Pretty. Smooth. I used to carve emu eggs. I used to do everything. Carved boab nuts. When I came down here this lady wanted about seven hundred boab nuts from Broome carved, and me and my friend carved them all for a pittance. But I enjoy art.

You learn all their habitats, where they go. Emus never lay eggs too far from the previous year. Like they have an area they go back to every year to lay those eggs. The turtles up in those creeks, how they survive God only knows, but I'd say they've laid their eggs and left them there over a time. Up further, on that Murchison, there's fish and it makes you wonder you know how they survived through the drought. The *bungarra* are fat during the winter. If you have the patience to go down there, and it's a hot day when they've been out for a feed — quickly and back in — you dig them out. Hours and hours digging them out, grabbing them by the tail and pulling them out.

Even too, what fascinated me was this Aboriginal medicine bush. In the old days they never boiled them. They couldn't boil them because they had no containers to boil them. I think that medicine bush was just soaked in the water. In the granites they have those waterholes and they go and get that medicine (refer p. 70–72). A lot of people, like in New Zealand, they get this healing water. Who knows if that wasn't the same thing that Aboriginals used, this medicine bush in that healing water? I do believe that it could be. There are trees underneath in the water.

That's part of my life that I lived. I lived right with them. I went out in the bush and learnt how to run along next to the horse and cart, trotting alongside. I was doing that in Morawa. I covered a few miles. That was part of it. Otherwise we'd walk for miles and miles. Sometimes we'd walk into town. The shortest way between two points is a straight line, and those lakes* we'd take from one point to the other. But they had water. We'd go from Morawa as a child for a picnic with an old billycan and a damper maybe or some sort of puffy piece of stuff. On Saturdays and Sundays we'd just walk about three miles [4.8 km] down to the lakes. But the fresh water was already there. My mother used to make gruel, she called it, when she was grinding up all the wheat. Yuck, that was terrible. But we had to eat it because we had nothing else, slimy blooming stuff gruel.

We cleared land in Morawa for the farmers, in the southern part of the town and the cemetery. That's when my mother got some money. We had no transport, and then when my mother had some endowment money we didn't catch the school bus back to Koolanooka. We'd stay in town until late afternoon to buy supplies and walk. We cut straight across the lake — it's only six miles [9.7 km] — and the guard knew us. If a goods train happened to come along he'd slow down and we'd all jump on. Then they'd take us the last part of the journey. But six miles, it's just small. Sometimes we were lucky we caught it in town, but sometimes we'd walk halfway. That wasn't too hard. Apart from that we didn't ask for nothing. It was where we shifted to when the Welfare first came and told us we had to get out of our camp on the edge of town.

On Thursdays, the old shopkeepers used to throw out their vegetables and their stale bread. Too much bread so they'd throw it away. My old Dad used to go there to the dump and pick up might be ten or twelve loaves. My Mum used to wet them, put them in the camp oven and they'd come out like fresh. Whatever we got hold of we ate. We used to eat yams, heaps of them. We'd eat them either raw or come back home and cook them in the ashes. We'd have stewed mushrooms, we'd have grilled mushrooms, we'd have any kind of mushrooms. I still eat mushrooms a lot today.

My mother and my aunty and my uncles spoke the language and they had visitors that came to the camp. My mother knew by some sort of warning or instinct and we had to go inside until she saw that everything was safe. I was a real sticky-beak. I used to peek because we only had old corrugated iron for our camp picked up from the dump. I used to peep through the hole in the wall and I could see Aboriginal people coming out of the bush. She used to talk to them in lingo, and when everything was fine they'd start the fire up and have a cup of tea or whatever they wanted, and we were allowed to go out and play. But previous to that we had to stay inside.

There was nobody, no other Aboriginal people for miles. The closest was some Ryder sisters. They came from Moora and Three Springs. I don't know whether they were Ryders actually, but their cousin was Johnny Ryder. The Bartletts moved from Three Springs to live in Canna Siding, which is halfway between Morawa and Mullewa. They had a camp there.

I used to go up there for a bit of a holiday on the goods train. Old Uncle [father] Norm Harris used to know all the guards. So we'd stand in the dog box we'd call it. Talk about a rough journey. They had a little room. Well the guard has the last carriage in those old trains, and in that carriage he had his own little office with good seats and he doesn't get thrown around much. We'd sit up there, and if we weren't careful we'd go clean off because there was nothing to hold on to. It was really only as high as a car roof I suppose. But when we were kids it seemed like a mountain and we'd climb up onto it.

My earliest memories

I can remember things. Even today I remember things that a million other kids would just forget in a lifetime. The soldiers I can remember quite clearly. They had these little dugouts all through the bush. We weren't allowed near it while they were there and when they did go on all you could hear was the clinking of their mugs and the rifle, and somebody saying, 'Left right, left right.' They marched all the way to Darwin I found out later. I don't know who was in it because I was too little.

I saw people after the war. I can remember them going through the streets with a loudspeaker and saying, 'The war is over. The war is over.' It was 1945 and I was born in '41. I can remember this man, I think I knew what it was, going through with a loudspeaker, a funnel-shaped thing. Everywhere we went in the street, people dancing and shouting and kissing one another, hugging one another, handing out beer and things to each other. Everybody was happy because the war was ended. There was everybody. They didn't stay inside. They went out, all joined in like to celebrate. We came from the bush but nobody minded. We were accepted into that town like white people.

The earliest I can remember, I was sitting on the ground and this roar came through the gum trees in the bush and then, following that roar, a deafening noise. The trees were just amazing and everything was shaking. It must have been an earth tremor because I looked up into the camp and I could see everything shaking. I told my mother and she said, 'No. You were too young to remember anything like that.' 'Oh,' I said, 'well how come I can remember seeing all these things?' I remember all the shaking. I was on the ground cos the ground was trembling. Anyway, I kept telling my family and I told my younger brother. He went to jail not long after, the last couple of years. When he came out he said, 'Oh, I found out when that earth tremor was.' He said, 'You were ten months old when that earth tremor actually happened.' Those people who were telling me I couldn't remember made me start to doubt myself. They didn't talk about it much but I knew I'd seen it. I can remember an earth tremor there and the travelling of the soldiers during the war. I must have been very small but it was pretty solid in my mind. I think maybe the fear of what was going on at the time made me remember.

I spoke to my older brother. I said, 'Do you remember an earth tremor going through there?' He said, 'Oh Christ yes. Everything was shaking, and the dog was howling.' I said, 'How old was you?' 'Oh,' he said, 'I must have been four or five.' I said, 'There you are. You're five years older than me.' Well I laughed, cos we were talking about this thing you know, about that earth tremor. I would have been ten months old cos the younger brother checked it out. And I was on the ground. I could remember looking up and the noise that came through the bush before the trees started going off. It was scary. I was only little, but I knew what fear was.

Memories from way back

Two ladies, Ann Harmon and Myrtle Harris, were telling me some of their memories from way back. That's seventy-blooming-four years ago. They were my first cousins. Ann was seventy-nine. She was five years old when they had an old camp at Rothsay. Their camp was made up of bags they whitewashed with some sort of liquid mix that kept the rain out. It was bags all around. The walls were made of bags. They must have picked up some bits of tin or something and they were living there.

Anyway, she went on to tell us they were really excited cos there were some girls, you know, to play with, they thought. They would have been a bit younger than them. Away they went next morning. They got up really early to see these girls, but when they got there the girls had gone. All they saw was where they had two fires once, and they must have camped in the middle of these two fires. They [the girls] covered all the ashes and everything up, I guess so that no fire would spread, and they'd gone along, cleaned it up tidy and went along. That was in *Rabbit-Proof Fence* but in the book, maybe in the story, not the film. They [the girls] didn't know the name of the place. They just went there for food and water. But that's where they got it, from my aunty and her husband and three kids. Well I thought that was just strange, that those girls happened to be the family from [*Follow the*] *Rabbit-Proof Fence*. Ann and Myrtle Harris were from Norman and Eva.

She's Ann Harmon now, but she was a Harris. But my other aunty was a Phillip, the eldest, right over there near Paynes Find. They used to converse with those Aboriginals there because we all spoke the same language. The Widi Mob is a group of tribes that all speak the same language. Myrtle was seventy-five and Ann was seventy-nine when they was telling me this. She's Myrtle Mullaley now but she was Myrtle Harris. Their mother was a half-sister to my mother. They had the same mother and different fathers. She was reared up with Aboriginals as an Aboriginal.

Anyway, when we first started I got them to do a bit of history of their life, what they thought, what they'd achieved, and how they got on in life and that. So we met with them on Sunday and when they started, well we laughed. We had some fun because they told us about everything. How they ate and — Oh, one said she wouldn't eat *bungarra* now, 'Oh yuck,' she said, 'we had it when we was kids. But oh no, not now.' Other one said, 'Why not? I eat it.' Cos her son's actually gone through the law and his partner was a full-blood and they had three children from Roebourne. So he was still well into that Aboriginal lifestyle. His children and himself had been through the law. So, yeah that was one part of the history making. It was just unbelievable. Oh they talked, and they talked, and they talked. Her [Mrs Harmon's] memory all came back and she said before that it was so, like, you know a forgotten thing. Mrs Harmon, Ann, she's been very sick and she's old. So is Myrtle but a little bit more lively. But Ann's like four years older than Myrtle and knows a little bit more, extra.

They also told us about other Aboriginal people around that we didn't see, only on rare occasions, and they would come from Yalgoo, Mullewa, Paynes Find, Perenjori, Three Springs, and Mingenew. Those same people all spoke the same language as my mother. I noticed in later years, in the book written in 1996 by Keefe called *Eastwood Ho*, that all the names through that area we've got under claim are Aboriginal words. I could pick up and remember a few of the words but as a child it was very hard. We were told to go away, not to listen to old people's business. But on many occasions they'd tell us the stories. During the summer we'd all be outside in the heat.

Funny times, flat tyres and travelling

I'll just tell you this off-hand. I had an old car and these people wanted a lift out to — her husband was working on the station [Kirkalocka]. I had no idea how far that was, 150 miles [241.4 km] maybe. I said, 'Oh no worries. Okay. I'll take you to my old uncle.' We went out there and his little cook and me, and anyway we had a flat tyre. The first flat tyre we fixed up. The next one blew badly. So me and this girlfriend walked ten miles [16 km] into the station. The station owner was really good. She said, 'Oh are the kids there?' 'Yeah.' She gave us cakes and things and gave us a lift back. 'Oh well I'll fix this tyre up,' the old boy said. When he had a look the whole tyre was hopeless. Ripped everything. Completely blown. We needed a tube and things. So we walked the same ten miles [16 km] again and she was kind enough to take us back again and away we went the next day. We slept on the road.

My husband's cousin — I'm just telling you about the funny times — he was a character. There was this old ute*. I don't know whether it was an old Ford thing or not but you know a real old-fashioned thing. No top. John his name was. He was deaf and dumb. But when he had a drink he could talk. Whatever clicked up top, and he'd laugh and he'd tell you yarns and things. Not properly, but you could never miss on understanding what he was saying. It was really funny. He used to have this old ute. He was never stuck though.

We went to get something and I said, 'Oh, I'll go with you then.' So away we went out too, it was only about twenty miles [32.2 km] I suppose, and he had a flat tyre. The next thing I looked, the tube was buggered and he was stuffing it with soft leaves. And the other tyre blew and the spokes — because they had wooden spokes on the wheels — and there he was sitting under the tree, 'You right, you right, just wait there,' you know, sign lingo. He made all the spokes out of the tree. Sat down he cut and he chopped them right down till they sat in that wheel. Away we went back to Magnet and it was getting dark and he said, 'Wait wait, wait wait.' Then he pulled up and he pulled out the hurricane lamp and put it on the front. We were bouncing along. It was really funny and he was telling me, 'No, we might run into kangaroos

2. In the bush

see.' If the kangaroo saw those lights he wouldn't hop in front of it. Oh he was a real character.

He was a Little. It was sister's and brother's kids. First cousin that was. Out of that family there were three deaf and dumb people. John Little his name was. Terrible funny chap he was. One of the younger ones, his brother I think it was, not long died. He went up to Carnarvon for years. He left Mount Magnet and went to Mullewa. From there he went to Carnarvon. You know I never saw him for twenty or thirty years and when he saw me he said, 'Ahhhh,' he said, 'where's this feller? Lennie, Lennie,' I couldn't believe it. He asked me all sorts of questions in his own lingo, but I understood because I'd got talking to him before. He was pleased, 'Oh look at the kids!' When he left them he said, 'They were only little feller. They're all big now.' I had some fun, I did. I did enjoy life at times. Didn't like the bashings. Got plenty of them.

Shifting from Morawa

I went to Morawa Primary School until we shifted out when the Welfare came and told us we had to get out of the camp. My brothers were eleven and fourteen then, it must have been, cos they went up to Mullewa and played cricket with the older blokes. It was the town team. They said, 'You're good enough to join the team,' because they were short of players and the boys used to go and practice with them, 'We're a bit short, two good boys.' So they went out there. One of them got a hat trick and the other made a batting, out of the blue. Well they really cleaned up Mullewa. It was a big story, these Aboriginal boys from Morawa.

It came out in the paper, 'Oh where are these kids living?' We were living in the camp in the bush and it was a sin I guess. From there Welfare came to Morawa to visit us. To this day I can remember these people coming to my mother's camp and, being a sticky-beak, I was hiding around the door. (We weren't allowed to talk.) I stood listening and I heard them say, 'If you don't go from here, we'll come and pick up the kids to go to Tardun Mission.' Well, we were gone. Tardun Mission* was always known to us as place of ill fame where the children were abused, and I knew it as that, and I knew people who were abused, half-fed, everything, a wicked* place. It was terrible. At Pallotine Mission, it was a bad place. They were not only abused by the priests, they were also abused by older boys. The girls were the same you know. Everything, the whole lot.

I knew this man — actually he was my partner for a while — and I knew there was something wrong with him. You know he'd avoid talking, and one day he got drunk and burst out crying, and he told us. The priests used to take them to Lancelin for swimming, and on the way back this particular priest would say, 'You can stay a little,' and he'd stay. Well, they abused him in the bush. And when they wet their beds they had to get up at four o'clock in the morning — cos it was too cold, no rugs, they had hardly any rugs in that mission — they had to go and have a cold shower. As soon as the priests saw them in the shower they'd rape them. That was going on for years, all the time. The girls were sent down here [to Perth] to have their babies. They taught them not to complain against the missions, homes for Aboriginal children, but I know exactly what they were doing. I mean they turned out to be gay, some of them, through no fault of their own, or bi-sexual or whatever you call it, and yet they were good people in lots of ways. You wouldn't believe. There's a lot of hatred of course for different people cos of what happened in that place, and I guess some of the victims were some of the offenders too eh. That was really sad.

Anyway my mother and my uncle and aunty would never have allowed us to go there, and that cricket was an opportunity. So somewhere out of that bush telegraph* or something spiritual, the old fellers came in from the bush, old Norm and Eva, and there was a big discussion. They knew that my cousin owned this old mud-brick house in Koolanooka and we had to go there to live. From there our Dad got a job on the railways in Perenjori, so Mum and the younger ones went to Perenjori and us three elder ones in the family went to Perth to go to school. I wasn't actually in high school at that time, I was in primary. We got sent down to Perth to go to high school. But when I came back from school I had to go to Morawa to my aunty. I never lived in Perenjori, only for a day or two. I came back eighteen months after I left for Perth. It was too much pressure.

Shifting around

I was so homesick you wouldn't believe what I was doing. I was walking in my sleep, and I dreamed that some Aboriginals were in a truck that I knew were parked out the front. I grabbed all my blankets and sheets and pillow, and I don't know how I steered through the store but I got through, and I was walking up and down on the verandah looking for them. But that wasn't the only time I'd walk in my sleep. I never ever settled down, because it was so strange and I'd never ever seen the city. I didn't know there was anything outside that world in Morawa, even when I got married.

I had to start making my own decisions when I went to Perth. I had no one to help me. It was like I was dumped there. And my aunty became my mother. When she left me all I had was these old pair of pyjamas and there was no elastic in the waist and they were boy's pyjamas. But I wouldn't give in. I wouldn't cry or anything and one of the girls helped me. I never had anything much, but they outfitted us in clothes there and when we came home we still had those clothes.

My mother used to make clothes for us when we were kids in Morawa, but we never had raincoats or shoes and socks. When we did get them we only wore them on Fridays when all the farmers came to town, so we wouldn't feel out of place, and a special little dress. When it was raining we used to walk in the rain. Otherwise we'd get a wheat bag and fold it from one corner to the other and it formed a hood. We'd have to go to primary school with that cover on us. When we got to school we'd hang it up when the other kids were hanging up blooming raincoats. But it didn't bother us because we were friends with all those kids that went to school. You know later on in life we remember it.

When I returned to Morawa on holidays I never went back to Perth. I went to Morawa High School after. I went down to Perth for first year and second year, half of second year, and then I went home. I couldn't handle it. I went back to Morawa to go through high school. But we didn't have a permanent teacher so there was no blooming great deal of things that I picked up, doing the high school. But those sorts of things happened, unbelievable. There were only about two kids that passed, got a Junior Certificate out of the whole school.

When I was living there with my aunt and uncle I did lots of sports. Netball they call it now, but it was basketball then. We used to travel from town to town playing the game against different towns in the area, all those places I mentioned before, Perenjori, Morawa, Mingenew. Koolanooka had a team. Mullewa had a team. That was the sporting part. I used to love tennis cos when I went to school down in Perth I learned to play it. I did well with it, but I never played it again after I left Perth.

I worked on a farm for two or three weeks. It wasn't long. I just helped this lady out. She had a new baby and they were really nice people. But the food was too rich. I ended up with carbuncles on my leg. It's just funny, but one of the little girls that I was looking after, helping her, is now a psychologist in Fremantle in the Education Department. I didn't get to meet her again but true friends you know. She was not a teacher, but one of the ALOs [Aboriginal Liaison Officers] in South Fremantle High School mentioned it to me. That was a good while ago, a good few years. We had stacks of fresh cream and porridge and milk and forever apples at that farm. Apples and cream, you know cooked apples, tarts and custard and cream. When we had porridge we had big spoonfuls of blooming cream on it and it really went to my blood. It left me with a whole lot of carbuncles anyway.

I was used to that sort of thing because when I went to Perth the same thing happened. I had an infection on my foot, and my foot was three times the size of the ankle part. I took the skin off when I was playing tennis. They were putting a new picket fence in and from there it got poisoned and infected. I was limping and I didn't know what. I was this little girl at twelve you know, limping around.

I met my aunty in town on the corner of Beaufort Street and Wellington Street. We used to call it Trichet's Corner, in Perth. There was a chemist there, Trichet's Chemist. I met her there and she asked, 'What happened to your foot?' I said, 'I don't know.' Oh, she was hopping mad. She came around to Alvin House where I was staying, and demanded to know why I was neglected and ra ra ra. Anyway I got to the doctor but I was two weeks off school. I didn't know it was so bad either. Then one night while I was asleep, it burst and there was blood everywhere. But it was so painful just before. The lady put my foot on a pillow. Her name was Mrs Pullen. They never used that pillow and sheets again. It was just blood, blood, blood.

She had a hostel thing. There were kids from all over the state there. I met a lot of kids and I still have contact with them every now and then. One turned out to be my sister-in-law later on. But they came from down south and we came from up north and, well the north stuck together and the south did too. But I still had a lot of girls from the sou-west friends. That happened down in Perth, and then when I went back to Morawa I worked on that farm after I left school.

Anyway I got a job in the Post Office, no worries, learning as a telephonist. Well the first three or four days it was a disaster! Those were the times you had to plug them in. I had people waiting for their calls for hours. I just got so confused I didn't know where I was. It was terrible. The phone never stopped ringing. And then that's when I got married.

2. In the bush

I didn't have a proper home life. I stayed with my aunty. She was really good to me, and the old boy, but I didn't get on with the cousins. So I shifted up to another cousin's place. Then they left there and I sort of left, wandered more or less from house to house sort of thing.

We had some rough times but in Morawa people were not prejudiced. The first day at school I punched into one boy for calling me a boong* and he was my friend ever since. Then after I left school I used to still mix with the same mob. But when I got married and went up to Mount Magnet it was a different thing. I never saw them again. Oh, now and then. I saw one in the casino one time, really good friends. They never walked past. They were good country people, the older people. It was so hard living in Mount Magnet — my mother had a camp up along the creek — but we didn't have to want for water cos we'd go down and dig the water out every day. Had to let it settle and take it back up in whatever we had, and use it for cooking and drinking. That was Mount Magnet. I had some good times in Mount Magnet. I learnt a lot. I learnt how to grow up. I was no more protected. I had no one to protect me and I was on my own and my husband was a bit rough, really rough. I learned to get over that.

3.
Raising a family

I don't know my skin name. My mother was stopped from all that talk because when they went to the [Moore River] Settlement. That's what they did. They tried to kill the culture of the Aboriginal people, tried to breed the black out of them. That's that, plain and simple. I think it's a pretty hard thing to do. Like they thought that in Widi country there was nobody left there, those people all gone. But we're still here and we come from that country. They just call it skin. You're allowed to marry a person from that tribe you know, that group, and certain groups you couldn't marry. That 'skin', that's a white man name, it's not Aboriginal. It would have been some other word. I haven't quite got the full story. My nephew knows and he could probably tell me what skin I am. I'd have to ask him then the reasons why, and how does he gets that.

It's interesting to know how they divided different groups. They had totems. Like when men go through the law, the group that they go with — it might be three or four people — they don't talk to them any more after. They're called *ngalanggu**. Quite often anybody who went through the law in the Widi area were *ngalanggus* to each other and they had to share their wives, or anything that another one wanted. They had to talk through a third party. You know, they weren't allowed to talk direct. It doesn't matter who they were. If they went through the law together they became one.

This totem thing is something similar. Depending on who they are. Maybe an emu can mate with some other bird or something. Before Aboriginals became people they were a bird or animal. It's always an animal. That's how we get the totems I suppose.

My Uncle Norm said to me, 'I want to try to teach you how to pick your husband, for your kids' sake.' He said, 'Whatever you do, don't

3. Raising a family

marry somebody that has some hereditary diseases.' I said, 'Oh well, what can it do?' He said, 'Well, madness.' Because everybody in those days was either mad or they weren't. There were no stress-related things and everything that they've given names to now, you know. You were either mad or you weren't. I don't know how you think about it because you're a white man [speaking to Bruce], but that's the way we lived our life.

I went down to Perth to find out there was such a word as stress. I said, 'What's part of stress?' 'That's what you've got.' That's what the doctor told me. He said, 'Sugar diabetes.' Well, lo and behold, Uncle Norm turns out to be my father. I didn't know that he had it and neither did he. I didn't know he was my father either. He got sick one day. It was so intense that he went from a big man to skin and bone. We found out he had sugar diabetes. Well I inherited it. I didn't find out until I was twenty.

To my knowledge the unhappiness only started after I got married. I was happy to be married, but the life was so different to what I was used to. I wasn't used to anything to do with married life I'm afraid.

Mount Magnet

From Morawa after high school, I met and married Lennie Martin (Leonard Michael Martin). He came from Mount Magnet in a football team. That was a long time ago, forty-eight years ago. I married him in Mount Magnet in 1958 and I had a couple of kids there. When my husband got an old car, an FJ Holden or whatever they call them, I used to drive around everywhere on my own, me and my kids. I'd go east and I'd go right around west and come back to where I left, all around Mount Magnet.

When I first got to Mount Magnet there were only a few humpies spread around the reserve, as they called it, made out of bush and twigs and this and that. Maybe one or two of them were lucky enough to get a tent, but that was rare. They were just scattered around laying everywhere.

Only a few people were in Mount Magnet. There was Eulie Campbell Ryan and her husband Jack. She went by Ryan but she was Eulie Campbell on her pension. Wiluna I think was where she came from, and then she went across to Wadjari country. Anyway, she and old Jack Ryan had a camp on the reserve. He only had one arm and they called him 'Left Hand Jack'.

There was Clara George and Ivy Warren. Clara George came from Mukinbudin. I don't know where Ivy Warren came from. They called Ivy's brother Balla Balla. That was his Aboriginal name. I think Kalgoorlie's where he came from. But Ivy Warren and Clara George had partners of two old Watson brothers, two old white men. Clara lived with two white men in the end, because Ivy died and the two old brothers were still in their camp. Their family told me, and they still say it today, that she came from Eucla. Apparently she was born with the name Sullivan — I don't know that for sure — but that's where the Sullivans come from, Eucla. A lot of people also came from Maralinga after the atomic tests.

Clara George was in Katanning and her children went to that Roelands Mission, so they didn't actually come with her. There were two younger ones, Gordon Nullagine and Roy George, but they didn't join her till quite a while after. I don't know where they were. Then some time later Percy George rocked up from somewhere on the Murchison. I think Murgoo. The rest of them were in Roelands Mission, except for Ollie George, he was working around on the station somewhere. He came after. I'm not quite sure when Ollie was there though. Clara's daughter Betty George ran away from the mission. She walked and hitchhiked. She came up there. They're quite a big family. But they came in dribs and drabs because they were coming of age, and they were sort of returning to their mother.

Albert Little and my sister-in-law [Jean Martin] were two first cousins and they had a family. But things were very poor and they were battling* for survival. She had a lot of children. She was really a good person but she got tangled up with her first cousin, as a lot of them did. The children came to know the country and to eat the same foods because of Clara.

Then there was Cauley Walsh. They called her Cauley Walsh but she was Cauley George. She married a Wadjari man. I'm not really sure if her mother was old Clara George. There were also the Fogarty family, my husband's first cousins, from Mount Magnet.

The Hedlums had moved on, apparently to Cue and Meekatharra. That was three of Polly Little's children, three daughters. Polly Little came from the other side of Meekatharra. Polly somehow ended up as Polly Polak. The only Polaks that anybody would find would be in Leonora, Kalgoorlie. Polly Little married a white man. The kids around Mount Magnet were Lily Martin's kids, Topsy Fogarty's kids, and Daisy

3. Raising a family

Hedlum's kids. They were the biggest majority in the town. Those kids were living there when I got up there. There was nobody else there much and they were more or less all living interlocking you know, all first cousins from everywhere. There were no other people in the town.

The kids from the Littles and Martins were all taken away by the Welfare to Karalundi Mission, the other side of Meekatharra. Burt Jean's kids went to Karalundi Mission, and the Fogarty kids were taken there too. Dorothy Jones's children, the Greens, were taken away. Victor Little's children were taken away. The eldest was sent to Moore River Settlement and the youngest to New Norcia. Polly actually died in Moore River Settlement. My husband gave me the whole story when he was alive.

The Welfare took lots of kids away to missions. Those children were reared up to what they learned was in the missions. It never came from their parents. Going out for *bungarras* and things, that's rare too. I mean, they all had mission-bred kids that live there now and some do go hunting and some don't. They'll eat kangaroo any time and they'll eat emu any time, but as for living a cultured life, like a traditional life, that's not on. Their immediate fathers and mothers didn't live it, although their forefathers did.

There's only one remaining old person who is Irene, about eighty-two or something. She's now Irene Harris but she was Irene Martin. She's my sister-in-law.

Then the Lawson's came along too. Two old fellers there called Ninghan Freddy and Ninghan Billy moved to Paynes Find from in between Yalgoo and Fields Find. There was a big camp there of Widi people. They stayed on Ninghan Station, Ninghan Freddy and Ninghan Billy. They didn't have any descendants. Ninghan Billy lived with one of the Lawsons, their grandmother or great-grandmother. She partnered him from Fields Find. They came down to Paynes Find. Walked I guess. When Annie lived with old Ninghan Billy, one of her sons, Billy Lawson, went there and married Mary Stack. There was one son by that marriage, Ronald (Ronnie) Lawson, and he died in 2007. They came from further down, Northam, York and all that, Ballardong country.

Ken Binder and his sister's grandfather lived in Three Springs, but their grandfather used to call in to my mother all the time and they talked in lingo. My mother and my Aunty Eva and Uncle Ken all had the same lingo.

There are two major creeks in the town of Mount Magnet. There's one east, and it flowed when the floods come down from Cue at the Breakaways; but it started at the top end, you know, Cue, Meekatharra. The rains, like this weather here, cyclone; you just saw a wall of water. The water came down the creek that fast it wasn't funny. If you didn't get out you were just bowled over. It came about three feet deep, but it was the speed of it! You had kids running along next to you. Well you're grabbing kids and getting out of the water. Where the two creeks met there was that much water on the bend — there was a bend coming down from Cue — and it missed the bend. It took the bend with it. It came straight down the main road. It was really frightening.

We were in an old house and that house was rocking. So my husband's cousin came up and they were there because their camp was all but flooded, it was in the creek, on the creek edge. So they came up to where we were, and all night they put a little stick in the ground at the doorstep to see if that water was rising, and it wasn't till four o'clock in the morning that the rising of those two creeks [stopped] and the water level. I didn't worry too much. I enjoyed the cyclone. I was used to it.

Having the kids

I have stray kids too I might add. The oldest one was a boy [Errol] belonged to Ron Simpson. Ron Simpson was just whatever you might like to call a ship in the night. Well he wasn't quite the first man, but he was a partner that I didn't live with. I never lived with the man but I got pregnant, and there was no such thing as an abortion those days. My husband knew. Len was my first partner. We were parted you know for quite a time. He was living in Mount Magnet. I was living in Morawa. I was working there and he used to come down.

So we got married and Len knew. It was like an agreement. Then there were Greg, Dean and Jenny. It didn't really last long. My husband was a good worker. He worked seven days a week not a problem. But he used to drink. When Greg was eight years old he taught him how to use a big truck and a front-end loader. Greg's never forgotten. He can drive them anywhere; can drive anything except an aeroplane or a train. He's got licences for everything. That's Greg. Of course my husband was playing up at the time and it was basically about the time we parted. He was a good worker and everything but he was a very violent person. That would have been somewhere around when I was twenty-six. We

3. Raising a family

myself, 'These birds don't want me up here.' So I turned around and I went back, and they followed me along right back to the edge of the swamp, where some people were living, then they flew away. Whether it was controlled by the old spirits or the Aboriginals or what it was I don't know, but I found it happened all the time. I was guided by something spiritual.

Old Norm had a lot of insights. He told me not to marry anybody whose family suffered inherited diseases. Well every time we talked about it and what did I do? I married somebody whose family's full of it. I went straight in and married a man I thought was wonderful. Ah it was a sad case. But sad to say he died. Too much drink. But one of the hardest working men you could ever find. He'd work seven days. He died in '74, thirty-three years ago. I had a short marriage but we still kept in contact. I had a very rough life and I was unforgiving. I couldn't forgive him for betraying my trust. We were better friends after we parted then we ever were whilst we were married. I'd help him the same as he'd help me if anything was needed. It wasn't a problem. That was Lennie.

When I ran away from my husband I was not very old, in my twenties. I was living in Perth, down here. I came down to my Mum's. We were there three years or so. Then my sister rang up and told me he'd died six or seven days before. Oh it was a bad shock, like a bad dream, but something that we couldn't turn away from. I can tell you this, that Aboriginal people suffer a deeper hurt than white people. That's something like Italians I guess. Where they're distressed they show their hurt. But blackfellers they don't. Some do, but people round my age hide it. It's a thing that we're taught to do. But young people they don't take long to forget. And I really think there's too much, mend our ways, 'ape the white man's ways, Our daughters are things of shame' (see poem p. 131).

Nobody died when I was young. Everyone was quite healthy until I was well in my twenties. In fact, I was forty-six when my mother died. About six years before that I think my aunty died. Well that hurt. And my old Dad, my foster father, call it what you like, him and my real father died. It didn't matter to me when Norm died. I was in Mount Magnet. I heard about it a few weeks later and I had no way of getting to the funeral. Norm Harris Senior was never my Dad, because he wasn't there to rear me up.

Giving up the children

After Lennie Martin and I parted I had three more children. I gave Stephen to a very good friend of our family. See I was trying to manage the first five kids. That was hard enough on my own. Then when I became pregnant with Sandra the same woman also took her, but something happened and the Welfare took them off her. The Welfare man met me in Geraldton and asked could he talk to me. He was very nice, but he asked me could a child just five months old fall out of a cot and break its legs and arms and ribs? I knew that that wasn't the case so I just said, 'No, that's not possible.' 'Well,' he said, 'we're going to take them off her, but we'll give them back to you whenever you're able to be housed.' The first woman who took them, she was all right, but whatever she did to Sandra I don't know. Sandra was a couple of shades darker than Stephen. I think that she was a little bit prejudiced with that somewhere. So the Welfare took them and they went to this other lady and they did really good with them. Housing's been a big problem with me all my life.

So I left them with this other lady who looked after them until they became teenagers. They were not adopted, but they took their last name. Excellent people. I couldn't have wished for a better foster parent for them you know. Leonie is her name. Leonie was their second foster parent. She was very good, her and her husband. She didn't have children when she got my two, but funnily enough she had two kids after that, a boy and a girl. She treats the kids exactly like her own — those kids were always reared up like brother and sister. They still are. She was white but a marvellous woman, marvellous people. Colour meant nothing. They reared those kids up as their own and eventually they parted. But it didn't matter, because they're still the same people to the children. Sandra was born in '71. So what's that make her — thirty-five. Stephen in '69 and Nicola in '67. There were no more children after that, and of course you regret having to part with two of the kids, but they were far better off with this lady than the others were. We had a rough life you know, battling.

I often thought about them and I did a painting of them, but I never brought them back. Stephen now, he's left. The Springs they were called, Jim Spring and Leonie Spring. Sandra still has a lot of contact with those two people, Jim and Leonie. They were excellent and till the day I die I'll be grateful for what she did, what I couldn't do. I gave up my right as a mother, to tell them what to do and I made it plain. I was old enough to understand that, even though it hurt me. It broke my heart. I knew that they had to have something that I couldn't give them.

Leaving Mount Magnet

I lived in Mount Magnet until Errol was twelve and the other two boys were a bit younger, about eleven and nine. I took off with my kids and I stayed in Mullewa with an old uncle, Victor Harris. But his wife wasn't very friendly so I moved on to another cousin's place. From there I went to Geraldton to my sister. I had to beg them cos we were homeless, and it was really hard to try and keep your kids alive. They were all right though. I made sure they were fed. There were no such things as vouchers and all that that they give you now. I think the first supporting parents thing I got was eleven dollars. Well I'd make that last. That was years ago, over forty years probably cos Nicky wasn't born yet. But we survived. They used to play cards. Well each week I'd go gambling, and I'd win this money and I'd fill the fridge up with that. Otherwise the kids would go down the beach in Geraldton and fish for the food. You couldn't go along to the welfare and say, 'Oh, could we get a voucher? We've run out of food.' There was no such thing. But anyway it was cheap enough to buy it, not like now, a hundred times worse. I used to get my two week stores for ten dollars. You know, it was hard.

I went back up to Mount Magnet and lived later on. Me and my husband parted well before that. But I wasn't really happy there. I still had no family around. I came down to Perth to my mother and I stayed here, and I've been here thirty years. But it never stopped me from going back home where I lived in Morawa as a child, back up to Mount Magnet and all of the bush that I went through, from Paynes Find to blooming Mount Magnet and all around Yalgoo. I still do the same thing. Sometimes I get very depressed because I sort of relive some of those bad things. The good times I try to keep hold of, but I get these flashbacks and they're gone. Still goes on. Soon as I get depressed I'm buggered. Everything goes haywire.

All the kids all ended up going to Geraldton High and living in a hostel, mainly because of the inbreeding within the town. All the people in the town were relations. When they were older I came down here to Perth, but they were in Geraldton going to school. Errol ran away, he didn't like it. I have to keep my kids out of that inbreeding. That was the reason I really left there [Mount Magnet], and anyway my husband and I were splitting up. I saw my children getting a bit bigger you know. That's not the way the law is, that inbreeding. It's not the law. But then you know, I started talking, making enquiries sort of thing, and they said there was no law against first cousins marrying, because nobody within the law thought that it would ever happen. But second cousins, no, not allowed. My granddaughter ran into some Sri Lankan bloke once, a taxi driver. He asked her, 'Do they marry the cousin?' 'No way,' she said, 'my mother would kill me. My grandmother would anyway.' See that's our family.

4.
My country

Wageral was the name of the tribe (or group) my mother came from. With other groups in the area they were all called the Widi group, because they spoke the same language. All these other smaller tribes with different names, they all spoke the same language and they all had the one law, and all the people were related in their own way. The languages they talk about, the difference is slight. It's easy for me to go to Roebourne and know what they're talking about, without speaking it. Or go to Kalgoorlie, you know exactly what they're saying. Also, when you're in those places, you develop the way they speak. It's uncanny but you can do it. You eat what they eat, everything; talk like they do. Up to Roebourne it's the same thing, everywhere. I've been over a big part of the Midwest, up to Roebourne, Kalgoorlie, Coolgardie, right up east of Mount Magnet, the north-east.

Yamatji* just means 'friend'. But within the Yamatji* you got all those people all the way almost up to the Kimberleys that are Yamatjis. They don't identify themselves as anything else but Yamatjis. And then you got them fellers up there in the Kimberleys, I don't know what they call themselves. They've got a different name. They're not Yamatjis. We sometimes call these other [Perth] fellers *yamatjis* (friends) but they're not Yamatjis, they're Noongars*. Like Wongis are Wongis. It's the same as us. They've got different areas, different names to their bands of people. But as one they are all Noongars here.

That's our country right through to the Lyons River on the coast. The Lyons River is Yamatji. The lingo is Yamatji. It was rounded off at the Lyons River, that's where it finished. They never fought amongst one another. They were in groups living in different places, but they were all brother and sister and what have you, and we respected them as our aunties and uncles and grannies and everything. But white exploitation and Native Title spoilt a lot, because a lot of the history I find has been doctored.

I was over in Adelaide in 1986 thereabouts — and before actually — I was visiting the museum. I never put a Native Title claim in until '97. It was really interesting if you go through all this history. I had a list of the people that came down from different places and were put into Moore River Settlement. Some were just a name given to them by somebody else. Some lived with their Aboriginal name, but not everybody. It was all that white input that gave them other names. There are other families that are Widi. Modern day younger people refuse to acknowledge it. But there were not too many, because they were from the Irwin River and the Greenough that was invaded early. They chased them out and killed them, perhaps the police files can tell you a lot more about what happened to the people. But the evidence of that country being inhabited is still there. It's like I was telling you about the waterhole (see p. 54). It's all there. It's unbelievable that those poor fellers lay around naked and used such primitive things to survive.

When white settlement started in Dongara and in the Midwest there, they shot and killed so many Aboriginal people, they drove them out of the area. All back there was our country. Mullewa people were my forefathers. That Wageral tribe was only ten miles [16 km] south of Mullewa. There's a burial ground there, and the whole business, belonged to the Widi people, or the Wageral people. There's one big burial ground in Dongara. There are other places too.

There was one tribe that came in when the settlers first came and they went to a farm. This is not a Dreaming story. It's true. They went to the farm and they were hungry and they asked them for food, and the farmer's wife and farmer said, 'Go down to the river and get cleaned up. Have a wash and then we'll give you a feed.' So they were happy with that and they went down to the Irwin River in Dongara — or a bit out of Dongara I suppose — and when they got in the water the farmers came along and shot the lot. Shot them dead. It's documented that a group, a small band of Aboriginals, were bathing in the river and a flash flood came along and washed them all out to sea. Well that wasn't the truth, because Aboriginal instincts would have told them the flood was coming and they wouldn't have stayed and waited for it. They would have gone. I'm not sure whether it's in the police files. The police files have a lot of stuff. That book *Eastward Ho*, I've got that particular part where he [Keefe] refers to the Widi Mob as the original people.

Those people all spoke similar languages. It's all been mixed up. All the names around that area there [the whole Widi area] come from the Widi language. But of course the old people died out and they got chased out, chased out from Dongara mainly, by farmers. You have to read some books and they tell you how far they chased them, 360 miles [579 km] east of Geraldton, and they were still within Widi country. That's a hell of a long way. But that isn't where it stops. It goes further, right to Lake Darlot.

Norm Harris's land

The Irwin River starts in Dongara. In my young days it was a million miles away, but when you get into the truck now, it's just a stone's throw. Morawa is eighty miles [128.7 km] away, but eighty miles is nothing. My family, my grandfather Tom Phillips, and that Wageral tribe walked that country. It gave them food, the honey from the trees, and all things that came out of that that fed us. The night porcupine — he comes out at night when it's cooler — he was one of the main foods. We were lucky to get a kangaroo, and that was only because old Norm had a block of land out from Rothsay, and he used to be able to do what he wanted out on that.

Norm Harris went to Rothsay — that's a bit of country out sou-west of Paynes Find — and he found some gold and had a show* [a mine]. It was strange because the block he had was 300 acres [121.4 hectares] at that time and a mining area was usually pegged out at about 100 acres [40.5 hectares]. But it was more near Perenjori when I come to think about it. So when he sold that show a bloke who came out from Perenjori bought it. He used to go out there working and collecting mallee hen eggs. More or less that was his livelihood. At last he sold it.

Anyway he cleared out the land to make the farm there in between Mingenew and Morawa, him and his brothers — he had a few brothers — Ted Harris and quite a lot of the old people. I wouldn't know their names. I just saw photos. Most were dead by the time I was born. He had that farm and the whole family used to come in there, and the government let him. But later on down the track it became wanted farming country and so the government wanted the land rates paid, and the land rates weren't paid because nobody knew anything about it. So they lost it all. The government took it. He was one of the early settlers in that area, but they lost all that.

All that area that I named, my grandfathers walked that country. My mother did too. They stayed mostly around Mullewa. That was their home ground. They'd come back to Mullewa. It was like a walkabout. Morawa was where I was born, not knowing what it was all about though. Dongara, Mingenew, Mullewa, Perenjori — all that there it's really familiar. The minute you go east; Paynes Find was a big part of it.

Remember when I was telling you about my Mum knowing when people were coming in to visit her? There were five people whose names always came up. That was Henry Sam, Billy Barlow, Ninghan Freddy, Ninghan Billy and Bob Redman. They would have been travelling through for business (the law). Ninghan Station was infested with porcupines and the Aboriginal name for them was *ninghan**. They say that Ninghan Station actually got the name from a black cockatoo. But that's where the name actually comes from, I say. I don't know what they call a black cockatoo, not offhand. But the *ninghan* is the same as Ninghan Station. Really the people from that country had the Aboriginal names from our lingo right through that area.

There is a bit written about that in *Eastward Ho*. Keefe expected all the Widi to be in Mullewa, the closest place. That's us. We're the living proof that that tribe existed because my aunty and uncles had family. Horace [Joan's uncle] took his family up to Carnarvon. There were six or seven of them. John [Joan's uncle] had those three and old Ethel, John's wife, came from Billabilong Station. She was called Ethel Billabilong. (They call the waterholes billabong there.) She used to go back to the Bowes River up the side of Northampton, and across to Cue. That's the other side of the Widi people. Ngalia people I think they are.

Breaking up the country

Widi was made of several groups, many small bands of Aboriginal people that knew the country so well. When the Widi Mob broke up into different areas, it was huge. The country went right over to Lake Darlot and almost to Coolgardie, all the same language-speaking people. It goes right to the coast from where I was, in our country. And they had to break it all up through the laws you know, different places. They had a big meeting and all the old elders went. That meeting was held either at Thundelarra Station — I always thought it was Thundelarra — but they told me it was Waradaa. Thundelarra is country that's got a heck of a lot of artefacts and things on it. Got a big creek there you know with all the tribes that came to it. So they had the meeting to break the country up, one was the western side like our Widi Mob; another one was to the north, Koara. You see it on the [Tindale] map. See the people went from Dongara — or from the coast there, Champion Bay, and the other part I was trying to think of was Jurien Bay — and go east. Our Dreaming comes in a certain group and they come on from Cue.

They broke it up so different elders looked after each area. My grandfather used to travel from the camp at the Irwin River all around the Paynes Find area. He worked for different stations but that was really why he was travelling. He had to go and check on all the sacred sites and things.

Tindale [anthropologist, Norman Tindale] was the first to map the Widi people. If you look at a Tindale map you'll see that he was the first one to map the boundaries. Tindale talked to thousands of people here. He went from town to town and bush camp to bush camp. I can remember when he came through Morawa in 1946, when I was five. His 'sole informant' for this area was a man called Amangu, and that was the meaning of it, Amangu. But it's not a tribe (see p. 158). He just said, 'Oh this is my country,' but his language and everything was Widi. They were all the same and Bowes River, that's Widi country all there. It goes from Geraldton right up to Cue way up past Mount Magnet, and that's part of the Dreaming track.

You'll see an arrow into different places where Tindale went. The arrows were put on the map because there was a flow-on. Native Title's based on what documents they put in at the time of white settlement, the anthropologist, the police, all that they had. They sent all those anthros out to document the sheep in the country as it were, because we were never recognised as people till '67. I get really depressed, knowing these things. Well all that country was named in Aboriginal names. But they were Widi. This is how the government has got everybody confused. When the kids go to those homes and things, it's easy to brainwash them cos they don't know any more. They never lived with their parents or the old people.

Tindale's map should show the Widi people all the way through to the coast. They come from that river, started at Dongara, the Irwin River and they took it right up to the Bowes River. There were always rivers and ranges and hills that they pinpointed, boundaries from that go all the way up there to Cue. That's where the water came down. When it rains the salt lakes and all that area fills up, but that water comes down from Cue. It's the Dreaming track. It goes right over to Lake Darlot. It should be all Widi. All encyclopaedias up until that date (1994) included Widi.

Eventually the Badimaia* moved in there [north-east of the Widi], and they took on the language. Now even today there are Wadjari people, Badimaia and other different groups all speaking mixed languages. But most of the languages are Widi, the words and names of things. Then of course, I don't know what headdress Aboriginals wore but they came out with a hat being a *maggawala**. It should be '*mugawala*' because that's the Widi name for head — *muga*. And if you've got a mental illness or something — a bit sick in the head they call it — then it's *mugayagu*. *Mugayagu* or *maggamagga*. Some things I can remember of the language, but it's got to come to me you know, because you weren't allowed to speak it. The people that were there were Widi. They couldn't converse unless they spoke Widi.

Wadjari people might work with one another and say, 'We got a young feller here we want to put through, when your law come.' Same as the others you know, they bring them along and they were accepted there, but not to the point of that person taking over any judgement on the land or making decisions on the country. The land must accept them, meaning the people. He can't claim the land. He can only claim where he went through the law and that. But apart from that he has no authority on the land. One man or woman you know, they don't have any rights to the land unless we [the traditional owners] give them that right to make decisions and things. They can't make their own decision on anything. Accepted be more to the point, they need to be accepted by the people. But if they weren't accepted well out they go. They'd be in exile.

There's no way a law camp was there on the coast. There were meeting grounds and travellers passed through, but there was no law. They tried circumcision but they weren't successful, so therefore there was no initiation in the coastal areas. Whatever law they're talking about was Widi law because Widi people — the language spoken and the connections — were right from the coast. Champion Bay in Geraldton up to the Bowes River near Northhampton, going east across the country to Cue, and further on to Lake Darlot, and probably almost to Coolgardie. Then down south halfway down to Jurien Bay and Dongara, that's one outlet for the Dreaming.

4. My country

Dreaming tracks

What we believe is the people along that Dreaming track own the country. That's why I know we come from Cue. The Dreaming track comes from there. The sacred sites and everything have never been Badimaia or Wadjari or anything. That's our Dreaming track and it goes right through to Dongara, Three Springs, Carnamah. When it rains in Cue, it floods and everything, it comes right down.

We don't like to tell everything. That's blackfeller, Yamatji's way. You get half the story, not all. An anthropologist [Ron Parker] kept asking me, 'Where's this water come from?' I said, 'Well it comes from Cue. Do you want any more?' 'No,' he said, 'I just wanted you to tell me that.' He said, 'I know where the other one ends,' and he said, 'what you've done, you've finally put in the rest of the jigsaw, and now I know a lot better.' He reckons it was one big jigsaw. There you are. He knew where that Dreaming track started, but I had to tell him because it's what I know. He couldn't tell me.

There were different groups and the Dreaming comes in a certain group and they come on from Cue. That's our Dreaming. You know they bring their Dreaming to Cue but that's where ours really starts. The waters come down from Cue that flood during the cyclones and everything, flood all our lakes and gutters and drains. That was really good.

I was there with my husband, just down from Cue at Mount Magnet. That's the Dreamtime you know. The hills, especially ranges, were always the Beemarra*, resting. They're all around. All the hills and those ranges of hills are the Beemarra. That's the big Snake. That's part of the Dreaming. But there was also the water, the salt lakes, and there were always these outlets of fresh water. It was common for Aboriginal people to follow that Dreaming track while living alongside the lakes, because there was always fresh water. Big lakes are there everywhere.

And the lakes — if you get on top of the hill you see the lakes are like a snake. It's the Beemarra track. The river is a Dreaming. You see the salt lakes and their winding track. But through time they've gone to salt lake instead of the river. That comes on to the river and goes into the ocean. You know your Bible tells you that God's everywhere. Well, to Aboriginal people it's not God, it's the Beemarra that created this and created that. I often ask people on which day did God create water? Cos there's nothing in the Bible that says which day it was created. So we've got that in our belief. I'm not saying I don't believe in God, cos I do — we got a spirit from somewhere.

All along that Dreaming track that I saw, in the salt lakes, there were artefacts packed all along the sides, and fresh water every now and then. So people who say there's no fresh water mingled in with the salt lakes, they're wrong, cos it's there. East of Mount Gibson is Lake Moore. My Mum told me many years ago when I was only little, there's fresh water in the middle of Lake Moore, and nobody believed me. Nobody believed that there was any fresh water anywhere there. Only last year we ran into this bloke who actually lives in the street opposite from my son in Hilton, and he came across talking about it and he gave us all these papers. I nearly fell over. I said, 'She wasn't lying was she?' It was all there, everything, all the mushroom stones and everything. I'd love to go back but I haven't been well enough. Each time we go, we go for a different purpose. I'd love to see it because I know my Mum wasn't lying.

It's marked clearly on the map that man gave us where all the fresh water was, and there are fish traps on the edge of the lake. There are piles of shells. There's everything. It must have been an inland sea at one time because a little bit further up you see the bones and things in the ground, fossils of a shark on Lake Barlee out from Ninghan Station. But, the time in it, you know. How come that was there, when the earth rose up or the sea went down? There's other things been found there, fossils.

Nobody hears about it because they don't want blackfellers to claim them see. Lets out too many white secrets. You know, all over the world they're digging up those sorts of things, but nothing's ever said about this. Beautiful Mount Gibson, a range of hills that in fifty years' time won't be there. Actually, there's supposed to be another bloke that was taking out hills around Morawa. That's where we come from. I said, 'You're taking the guts right out of our country.' Money. Money makes the world go round maybe. Also destroys everything. I can't go along with it.

Our Dreaming starts from Ernabella and it comes across, four serpents, two male two female. The one that comes in the Midwest was Beemarra. They were called Kuniya*, those snakes, but ours were Beemarra. They were Kuniya when they left from Ernabella. There's different names in the north. I'm not sure what they called it over in Kalgoorlie way, but they'll have their own name for these fellers. I know that Dreaming track comes across from Uluru to Yakabindie. That's where they sent across the Beemarra to look after the Aboriginals. Yakabindie is where they split up and went in different directions, part of the Snake Dreamtime. There are seventy-five sacred sites on that one hill. They had completely different names in law and when they came to us in the Midwest it was the Beemarra, and when they came from over the east there was a different name. I know the name but I can't think, only what they call them here, Wagyl. They were Kuniya like I said, and a lot of them have the Rainbow Serpent up north. But they've got another name, Kullark or something like that. There were two male and two female. So those two males and two females must have had offspring eh, and you see that hill arrangement could have been and would have been part of the Beemarra anyway because of that, male and female.

There's lots of little things I've been taught. You don't tell people everything. They'd talk about that Dreaming because it belongs to Aboriginals, and the medicines. I couldn't put a name on a medicine bush but I know what they are, and of course whitefellers have got so many names to fit so many things it's confusing.

If I take you there I'll tell you, but try to put it on a map, it's confusing. Like the Bible says you know, there's the Father, the Son, and the Holy Ghost. That spirit, the Holy Ghost, we've got something so similar to the white man's version of the beginning and the end it's uncanny. That Holy Ghost is just there. It's never away. The Beemarra is everywhere, and the Bible says God is everywhere. You know what I mean? That's how closely they were related. God is everywhere, well so is the Holy Ghost and the Beemarra.

The Beemarra came to us across a wide part of the land, from probably down here past Eneabba, further down south, from there up to Bowes River. Cos the rivers and the lakes and the hills are boundaries, they form boundaries. But right up here it goes to the Bowes River and down and right across to those other places I was telling you about — Lake Darlot, past there nearly to Coolgardie. See they got Kalamaia language there, but those people, you can go anywhere and you can understand that lingo. It's only a slight difference.

There's a berry bush at Mount Gibson. I used to eat those berries when I was a kid. Where we lived in Morawa they all disappeared. There are little flowers before the seeds come in. A beautiful place this really, Mount Gibson. I haven't been there for ages, four or five months or so. Mount Gibson itself is a sacred site. The rock has a double face, a change of face that's around it at the waterhole there. You can see eyes. That's only one of the faces towards you.

Tallering Peak is where they're mining. Hundreds of people used to go there and go through the law and the blood comes from around here, that's where they shed their blood, and the tribes and all the ghosts of the elders live there. That's just how I sort of put it, because they came from east, west, north, and south. They came to go through that law. There's the old people watching what's happening, and their blood was there. It's better when you see it for yourself, to tell the story.

It's all here at Mount Gibson mine. These are the little lakes or whatever. We got the map off that bloke. He was working there. I didn't know anything about it, and I often wondered cos we knew a story about the *dunart** [kangaroo mouse]. They used to tell us about the Dunart and the Bungarra. Well that must be where that came from because that's where the *dunarts* are. These animals they're unbelievable. They did the survey for tourism I think, but nobody goes there, very few. Our Dunart's somewhere there. I got so much stuff through the years. See, it's nine, nearly ten years I've been mucking round with Native Title. But it just seems to happen that quick, I'm lost in time. I mean, it seems like it was only yesterday that I was talking to you.

On the edge of this Dreaming track are granites hidden up by sand, salt and lakes, lake country. They're all along lakes, the granite rocks. They say, 'You go out to granites.' Not one particular place. They're all around. They pop up. See granites contain water. They soak it up during rains and it runs off into the lake at any time. There's a thing out there, a huge granite you can walk into if you were skinny (not like me), and you can go inside. The people have names for them. Only the people that know the name talk about it all the time, but I can't think what it's called.

I was really excited when I went up the bush about eighteen months, two years ago, and my grandson found a waterhole. It was still there, it's permanent, and there were thousands of artefacts. You could almost picture the old fellers that lived there before and how long they lived there, and how big was the tribe that fed off that water and trapped their meat. It just runs through your mind. It wasn't always boomerangs and spears that killed them. There were other things. It's just so old that place.

4. My country

One of our sacred sites is a granite that's flat and it looks just like a perfect damper with a wedge blown out. The interesting part is another round rock, perfectly round, behind it and they say evil spirits come out of that rock. There's a permanent waterhole where the boys got hold of a *bungarra* and they were cleaning it. The water was coming out of the top of the hill and dripping down into that waterhole. It's hard to believe that water can run off the top of a hill permanently, for years, through the drought and through everything else. It looks green. Changes with the weather I think.

A waterfall came out of that rock and it went into another little split, and from there it went on into a little pool, like there were three steps where the water busted in. That's the one also with the stone. You know it's got a stone in it to keep it clean I was telling you about (see pp. 61–2). But once that mining company gets hold of it there'll be nothing. Nothing, and we won't see anything again.

These were the sort of things that were always there, the granites. People don't regard them as anything special but they hold plenty of secrets. They have camping grounds. They have caves where people have obviously lived in the shelter. Like we were on a hill here and that's the road. This is a line of iron ore. I don't know what they call it, magnetite. It runs straight along the hill and runs to a big sacred site.

The mining companies about these sacred sites — well, especially one — they're very helpful. They don't want to go around destroying people's sacred sites and things, because that's their way of working together I guess. A lot of things are there that you wouldn't believe. The stones that the old fellers put in place many years ago are still there. Because when they came in and pushed the Widi Mob out, those people went into the country more. In and in they chased them. *Eastward Ho* said they chased them some three hundred miles [482.8 km] in the bush, and found them there. I'd love to have that pinpointed, the exact spot where they caught them if that was possible.

The fires that go through the bush create a new growth of vegetation. The vegetation is different and it's very thick in places so you're hidden and the sites are hidden. But I don't know whether that's nature or what, or a protection for Aboriginal people's sites. Because you don't see it until you walk right onto it. I mean those sites don't have to be standing out in the open. They can go very low on the ground and you have to crawl in maybe eight foot [2.4 m], and you can't walk back. You've got to go on your hands and your stomach under the granite because that opening is only just big enough for you to get through and you can't turn around. You've got to go all the way right through or back out the same way you go in.

A bloke from New Zealand took his woman in there. He's a modern day blackfeller. They were working at Ninghan Station and he went in to Paynes Find on their day off, bought a block of grog or something like that and went for a picnic up in the hills. Just by mistake he found that opening in the ground. He shot a kangaroo and it went through these granites and then he noticed this tree. He thought the kangaroo got past the tree. But then when he looked he saw a little shelter on the bottom of the hill, but it was a hole. Being half drunk, he put this woman in it and said, 'Go and have a look what's in there.' She said, 'Oh, I'm game.' So away she went. She had to crawl eight foot [2.4 m] and she reckoned that inside were all sorts of things. She couldn't explain them to him. You could walk around inside, but she came back pretty quickly. She was afraid of snakes and traps and things, cos he'd warned her. I daresay that's still there but who's going to walk along and get into that cave? None of these modern day blokes that reckon they know everything would dare go in there. You'd have to put some sort of a thing in there like you see in movies, feelers to see what's happening. That's where there are sometimes booby traps. Because if you're not allowed in that place, then there's one thing that Aboriginal law did was kill or cure.

Signs

Another thing that we saw that's in the bush was tall gum trees in our country that had shields shaped out of them. I was so dumb I said, 'How come they're so high up?' I never thought how long ago it happened. The tree grew. It was really funny. I go past that all the time because it's in farming land and it's so visible, from outside the fence. I was thinking seriously of having that area recognised. I mean there are dead trees, a couple of them, but they still got that cut-out in the wood over so many years, and half circles of stone.

I've had a bit of an argument to claim a whole region. It's the same as painting. We're painting here by ourselves and painting is never done — not from our way — from our point of view, because it was all done as everybody. The ones that they did in the cave they had to go back and touch them up. It's marvellous but I read in the paper, comments to the editor, where if they were done so many hundreds of years ago, how come they still look fresh? They're touched up. There are some people they call the 'line cutters'*. Well they've got to check on all that, and the waterholes, everything. That line goes all the way across to the east. From Ernabella the Dreaming track went to the centre.

My son was over there. He went on some sort of thing with a group and he climbed up on top of the rock. He got up there and he took all sorts of photos of going up there and coming down. He quickly went and got them developed. Or so he thought but there was nothing. Nothing came out, and he asked the old feller there, 'Why didn't it come out? It's a good camera.' The old feller just put his hand on Greg's shoulders and he said, 'You right boy,' he said, 'You belong here. That's why. This is your country too.' So, you know, he said he felt the hairs on his neck going, cos he wasn't allowed to take them, something to that effect. That's what the old people told him, 'You right boy. You belong here. You come from here.'

I've been to places where no grass would grow. Would be about a good twenty metres, twenty-four metres or something like that. That's the radius, and you can almost see the tracks where they dug it into the ground to do their corroborees, and the stones are there in a perfect circle. You know a thing like that you don't just walk on to anywhere. It's a sacred site. I mean it's a fact that wherever there's fresh water is a sacred site. It's not a coincidence. It's not just what somebody can name as a sacred site or anything like that. It *is* a sacred site.

There are other things I'd love to know some more about. There's a big thing there in Dongara. I've seen it somewhere in a book where these stones are put in an arrow shape. I think it might be in *Eastwood Ho*. It's just that I know there are other things between Morawa and Mingenew and Dongara and I could never get back. I've been all around Morawa up the different roads. I've never come across it again, and I haven't been back for years. I was a young woman — not young, about thirties I suppose — when I last came across from Mingenew to Morawa, but when we were kids we used to travel there. My mother and my aunty used to dance, corroboree dances with fire sticks. We lay down and you'd hear the people whistling. You'd hear the bush noises that you expect to find out of a lot of people. Uncanny, but it's there. All those things, and there's things that I haven't got back to see. They wouldn't let us go to this hill. They said, 'No that's Mundong Hill. You can't go there.' And the creek itself was dark and the bushes were growing over, 'No that's bad, and this is bad.' You know, we weren't allowed to. The only way we knew it was there was cos we were travelling through.

When I was little we only had an old horse and cart sometimes. Some of the oldies had an old truck or something and we could run as fast as the truck. We used to run alongside it. It was good fun. We'd go from Morawa to Dongara every year without fail, whether it was at Easter or Christmas, but we'd be there. And there were places that we walked and steered off, 'You can't go there, come this way.' We had to walk close to my mother. She knew lots of things. She talked Aboriginal all the time when no one else was around. A lot of times she whispered. My old aunty did, all the time. She shifted to Perth thirty or forty years ago. That's where she whispered. She never wanted anyone to hear her. I used to go and visit her every day because she was sick. Birds were there and it was as though they were listening, and they found her every day of her life.

We went the other day and saw the Irwin River. There were beautiful trees and clean sand, somewhere you'd really like to be. You could live your life there if there was a shop close by, because everything there means peace, but we've become accustomed to the food we eat now. I mean you'd have kids running everywhere for food in the old days. They'd be running catching lizards and whatever, digging *bardies** and everything, and it's so pretty that place. You could understand why my family and all the other little mobs, you know, little tribes, they were no different. They were all the same group but different groups of people lived all along that river, and really it was a Dreaming track, and the people who come off those Dreaming tracks where the salt water lakes and all that flow from are the true people. Well Native Title for instance, you know they look for the people that belong there. The ones that come in from the desert, well they've got a different way, different living.

It's just uncanny that they knew all these things long before white settlement, and look at just two hundred years, call it what you like, but it happened. Those people knew those things and of course they passed a lot on. I was lucky. I used to listen and I was a sticky-beak like I said before.

Native Title, mining and government

I saw everybody going mad over Native Title in Adelaide when we were gathering our family history at the Adelaide Museum. I came back over here and they were talking about Native Title and I had all of this history. There were a lot of books actually and we were putting it all together for that purpose. When that came around I said, 'Oh gee, I might throw a spanner in the works.' All the Native Title was set and sealed and there was nothing more, and what they said about this that and the other was gospel. But I had the papers and the proof and I knew it wasn't gospel. It's all Widi country right from the coast across, but Native Title changed a lot of things. People got greedy and they imagined you'd be millionaires out of it or whatever. But it was never meant for that. It's so unbelievable that these people think they know all about me and my family and they're using it against me. Some people put in the wrong story. Well you know, whatever they think is gospel, so long as you're white. If you're white you tell the truth, if you're black you're a liar, and that's common. It's most important for everybody to see how worthless Aboriginal people are, because the mining companies are fighting us for the land.

During this mixture of Native Title and the madness and the corrupt land councils, they brainwashed them into believing things that weren't true. They start off with the working party like, willing and able young people. It's really hard to understand why anybody else would claim country that doesn't belong to them. I can't understand that, when they don't know those places and what meaning it has. Then the whitefellers come along with their mining companies and they mine it, so everything that's in those hills is destroyed. But very deep down there are a lot of spirits from the older people. That's what the court fight's over. They want to know how much we know about the country, and what kills me is they don't know anything and they're letting mining companies dig up our heritage. It's not their heritage so why should they worry, you know? That's the sad part of it when you've got to talk to mining companies and they say, 'Oh no, we had to show them what an artefact was.' [Meaning they showed the local people what their own artefacts looked like.]

They're all touchy I think [the people in the land claim]. They're very frightened people because of this Native Title that came through here, even though they're going to appeal. Why would they appeal when they know we are the original people? This is genocide* isn't it? It's creating genocide. We didn't have to have money before whitefellers came. We didn't have to search for water because our water was there, and our food was there. We didn't have to drive cars. We didn't have to do those things. Oh it's convenient, but at the same time they're denying us our rights.

I don't think any treaty that's ever made between Aboriginals and whites should go through and make mining laws, and let this government claim what's under the ground and all those things that matter. They reckon oil and gas and everything that's under that ground belongs to them. How can it? How can somebody give us the sand on the top, like they did here, but nothing underneath? This freehold business is a load of rubbish.

What annoys me is I reckon the government allowed some mining companies to destroy proof of our existence before the anthropologists came. All those sacred sites are getting destroyed through mining and the things they did in the farming industry. And you look at the government making all sorts of claims. It's heartbreaking because I've lived that life. I've lived it for so long and I've been getting so sick and I'm getting older. So you know where does it stop? In this Native Title we have to prove we're the original Aboriginals. Yet we're not white. ['You can't be white so you can't prove it in white ways.'] We can't line up the same as a non-Aboriginal because we're not. We're not Asian, we're not American, not anything else but Australian. Not Australian. We're not even Australian; we're Aboriginals, the Indigenous people and it's that hard to tell people. The terrible thing is that I have to prove where I come from.

5.
Caring for the land

Through my life I had a lot of experiences with different areas. I found little waterfalls that I never knew about. The other people up in the country knew, but I come onto them myself. Sometimes beautiful little waterfalls and the rocks had been worn and you get those little river-like rocks you know, smooth. Pretty little places. Those waterholes all around Morawa and that, they fill up, cos the water comes down after the cyclones. Roads would be washed away. They always have fresh water. The lakes may be salty themselves but there's fresh water all along it, otherwise they would never survive there. Aboriginal people couldn't survive on salt water, but they had ways and means of doing things.

Sometimes the waterfalls were a couple of metres but not much, because time has worn them away. The waterfalls I was going to show you are a bit higher, up the hill a bit with all the green grass growing on top. When my grandson went there after a couple of years he said there were five emus, and one a bit younger must have been last year's chick or something. But he said they ran away. They were feeding there, but when he came back, they came back. They did a full circle. They can move straight back, not afraid. Emus aren't afraid to do anything. It's weird I tell you.

After going into their country and seeing for yourself, you know, they'd never be short of water. It was there. Beautiful, and there's this one sacred site. It's coming out the side of a small hill, wasn't a big one. It's running out and it goes back into the rock and comes out into a little pool, and in that pool there's a big round stone. This is how we know it's Aboriginal. That round stone was put there to purify the water for blackfellers. They put it in that water where it's running and it keeps fresh all the time as it comes through, Aboriginal magic or something. They were clever people. I mean the water's permanently fresh.

But there's so many waterfalls it's unbelievable, and Aboriginals could walk that country and never die of thirst. Water's the only commodity in the world that every living creature can't do without. That's how it is. Lots of things happened that Aboriginal people have that knowledge. They know when to shut up. They know when to talk. So when you see any Aboriginals here running amuck and carrying on, you know they don't have any idea at all.

All those granite stones, they're everywhere. You have ironstone hills, but then the granites are part and parcel, a runoff. And because granites are porous and they can collect the water, some of those granites are hollow inside and you can actually hear it ringing when you pat the top of it. But we know also that there are certain places to get in to the biggest granites. When you get in there you'll find a big pool, bottomless, of fresh icy cold water.

Gnamma holes* [hollows in rocks that collect water] are only small. Some of them can be bigger. I don't know who gave that name to them. Of course people don't know what the name is mostly, and of course there's too many years since that happened. Stolen generation and missions have stopped that language from going on. Not only language, the law and the culture too. I mean people are lucky if they've got some old people to talk to. You can go anywhere in the north of Western Australia, in the Murchison area, and they can help you and tell you. I used to have a lot to do with different people and finding out myself. I saw a big corroboree ground and inside that circle of stones there was not a blade of grass. They powdered it up that much nothing would grow on it. It was just open. In your mind you could see them dancing and corroboreeing around there.

Hunting and bush food

Aboriginal people bury their weapons and their boomerangs and all that under the fires. They did that all through the lakes area where they made a fire, they didn't carry them that much. Maybe a spear or a boomerang, digging sticks, but it was an overload — if you understand that — and they'd leave most of them, because they'd move on to the next place and get another lot. But where they buried them they'd go back. They'd know that was there and they'd go back and use it again. It was the only brainy thing to do. You're carrying your kids and a couple of things, maybe odd things to use on the way. They knew the same implements were there for the next use, and there and there and there. At the same time they were tempering the wood underneath the hot ashes. You know people do other things. They rub oil and all that. Well that was another way, for most of the times they used that heat from the fire. They'd leave them in those caves under where the fire was and it would cure them as well, the heat.

There's a nut that gets carted around. I thought it came from up in the Western Desert or the other side of Wiluna where these big trees grow. They brought them down to our country. This tree come down from the other side of Wiluna, but they must have brought the seed in their travels and planted them, cos there were five at this one place. Little yellow, orangey coloured nuts. They'd crush them and block all the waterholes off at the granites. They'd block all the other waterholes off and leave one, so the animals had to go to that one waterhole in an area, you know, where it's pretty dry. They'd put some of this crushed nut into one of the waterholes that the kangaroos and emus use. Well the emus and the kangaroos would go away and they'd fall fast asleep. But it was not only kangaroos and emus. It was any sort of animal life that they could eat. It was like a drug.

Up the north they'd dope the fish. Crush the same sort of stuff from a tree — I'm not saying it's the same — and knock the fish out and just gather them up. That's how they did it. It was as simple as that. They'd shove this thing in the waterhole and they'd go away and lie down and sleep. Easy meal. It was clever because they knew exactly how much of this drug to use. They didn't kill the animal and he was still good to eat. It's something that people found out much later you know, like you have anaesthetic. I mean, this is millions and millions of years before white power or settlement or scientists and all that came. These people were aware of it. If they put too much in it would probably poison them, but these people knew how, when and how much. How clever were these people that have no credit for their knowledge of survival? It really spins me out.

I tried to make a list of all the bush foods. There's mainly the kangaroo but we only ate what they call *marrloo**. My mother ate the *biguda**, which is a rock kangaroo. They can hop all over the hills. But I didn't eat it. I had my own instincts. Those kangaroos were muscly, tough little fellers. Not little fellers, they could grow quite big. Little muscly sort of a kangaroo, but it had yellow fat and I didn't like it because it was too tough. But she used to love it, my Mum. She reckoned they always used to go for the arm of a kangaroo. That was their sort of delicacy. But we were *marrloo* eaters, the reds you know.

There were some western greys* but we were a bit inland off that western grey. The western grey is a coastal kangaroo and when he hops, he hops straight up and down. Must be to combat with the sand in the hills, and he was different, quite big too. But most of the kangaroos we were allowed to eat, because we were living more or less on our own. The elders said that if they were at a tribal place we couldn't eat the tail, the heart, the kidneys, the liver, or the brain. The men eat the tail, the fat, the heart, the liver and all that — the delicacies as they call them — and the women just have to be in the background and eat what they can. The head of the kangaroo was a delicacy meant for the men and the elders, the fat too. They were fussy about that. That was in the big mob, in the tribe. We were all right because we weren't in the tribe, but my Mum was and she said those things were what they call delicacies for the men, the hunters. I wasn't in the tribe but just what I was told.

You couldn't eat salt. Those things were for the men. After the men get their special treats the women and kids have the rest. The salt they get comes from the lakes. Blackfellers eat it with their meat. I can't tell you the name because we don't name the lakes out from Morawa. You know whitefellers name them but we don't. Of course this is any lake salt. Not allowed to eat the salt. It was an insult for Aboriginal people to put salt on their meat. It meant a certain death.

When civilisation came in it gave a new meaning because there were such things as salted meat, and they did have that. They carried meat like white people keep it. Aboriginal people did it for a long time before white people. I know a lot of people that salted their meat and hung it up. Like these fellers they salt the fish. My mother-in-law actually used to do it, and when they were out on the station her and her partner they'd send it in to me, and it lasts for ages. It was the best kangaroo meat you could get. That's when I was living in Mount Magnet.

We could track the porcupine when we were kids because their feet are back to front. People go and track them and you think they were walking the other way but they're not, they're going forwards. But they were poor little things. When they roll them over and hit them on the head they'd cross their two hands in front of their face, in front of their eyes. When they cooked them and ate them and that, there's a cross on the back of their neck. What it meant I don't know. Donkeys have them too, cross in the bone. But back of the neck it makes you feel funny. We used to love those porcupines. They were easy to get. During the spring you know when the ants are just coming out; you'd always find them digging in the trees.

Anyway that kangaroo was the main part. And emu, the eggs, the meat itself and it's often cooked in the ashes. They say ashes but it is really heated sand. If they killed an emu and they just give it time to set, it was like chicken. No different to chicken. That's cooking them whole. But the eggs, they used to eat the eggs, every part of it. Legs, the gristle in the legs and feet I don't know what, but they were a delicacy as well, stomach, and the backside of an emu was a big fat rump.

At different times — well I said I was a sticky-beak as a young person — me and my kids we'd pick up things and go kangarooing, or take the dogs and grab an emu or something. We'd sit down in the bush and learn. Sometimes it was my Mum, or an old friend that befriended me when I went up to Mount Magnet. She was very close to me, showed me how to cook the emu gizzard. You just grill it, but what I had to do to get to it! I mean you had to pull all the insides out and the top layer, the stomach lining, before you came to the sweet meat, and grill that. Kangaroo stomach. Kangaroo guts we used to call it. Grill that. And the liver was sort of a delicacy for people. I could understand why because it was really sweet meat. They had certain pieces of stone that had a serrated edge which you could use to widen any cut. I mean they were well informed. They knew everything.

Duck eggs and ducks and things that were around. They called them mountain ducks. I don't know what the white man's name is, but they were pretty birds. They'd nest in the trees and there'd always be two holes, one at the top — one to go in — and one to fly out. So what we did was block the top one off, and then put your hand in and you grab the duck there, kill it and eat it. I mean it was easy to rob a duck's nest. Mountain ducks round Morawa, everywhere round there, those blokes.

The bush turkey has one partner for life, did you know that? And when you kill one you got to kill the other? When you shoot or you kill a turkey's partner, the other one cries. It doesn't make a noise like a bird. It makes it more like a human crying and it runs round and round on the ground and it flaps its wings, really distressed. It's really sad. But until you kill that other turkey that one will stay there, fly around and round and round. I have a cry for that poor thing. I didn't want to eat it. That's the turkey, but it's also something we could live on. They follow the grasshoppers, insects. Wherever they are in plagues, always you'll find the turkey. I painted a big one of the turkeys and I didn't really like it, so I sold it and I came up with another one.

They ate swans too in the old days, but they reckon it was the toughest meat they ever had, not good. Up there there's quite big lakes and they got swans on them. We went out there catching the eggs. Not catching them, they float on little nests in the water. That country is some way from the coast out east.

The pelicans get caught there because they can't get away. Some lakes, unless there's a lot of water, they got to stay there. There's all sorts of fish and things. There are fossils out there, fossils of a shark on the side of Ninghan Station, on Lake Moore and Barlee, fossils of fish. And they have fish traps on the other side of Mount Gibson, on Lake Moore's edge where they did fish traps, something similar to the people who live on the coast. Sometime I suppose there were inland seas as well with those huge lakes. They have a tide as well controlled by the moon.

Mating time's over for the magpies. I don't know what they call them up here but we call them mickey minors* in Morawa and around about. There are plovers there. You'd never see a plover now. We used to go and collect the plover's eggs and you'd just never see them. The same as the berry bush, you'd never see a berry bush that had been dug in. I used to go every day for those birds.

The old *bungarra,* he was a delicacy too. *Bungarra* can grow up to a metre and a half long, nearly two metres. When they're opened up all these *bungarras* had yellow fat, and these other fellers have white fat — oh turn you off even more. On the side of Granite Hills they have lizard traps. But lizards are a modern day name. You know it's a white man's name, lizard. But we just go along with that flow and call them lizard traps. They get a flat piece of granite held up by a little rock underneath, and they'd chase these *bungarras* until they go under that rock, then they'd kick the stone out. So it was an easy way, because of course they're not frightened of *bungarras* and lizards and things. They put their hand in after. So long as they're trapped, they don't waste their breath chasing them. All over those hills and granites, in that area there are lizard traps galore.

There are plenty of *bungarras* and we used to call these lizards *djubbies**. The little ones were called *djubbies,* and the *bungarras* of course are the big ones. That black *bungarra* we did not eat. There was another one called the Diamond Head, very pretty feller a Diamond Head *bungarra,* shaped like a diamond and had a lot of black in it. I know somebody who ate it. We wouldn't eat it. We were taught that the black *bungarra* is the law maker. Nobody ate him in our mob. I often wondered why, but that's what we were taught.

There's a certain place east of Morawa and the coast that just breeds black *bungarras,* and they're savage. That's another sacred site called Willara Flats on Widi country in between Mount Magnet and Paynes Find. It only has black *bungarras*. There were hundreds of them and when you go there — cos there's a whole flat — if you disturb them everywhere black heads pop up. We never ate them because they were really arrogant. If you disturb them they run. Of course there's no big tall trees there. They're flat, and if anybody stays around you know, tall, they run up that person and scratch them and everything trying to get away. That happened all the time to an old lady I knew. She was dead scared.

But it's hard for *bungarras* because they can only run a certain distance and after that they got to stop. You can easily run them out and they've got to go up a tree or in a hole or something. A hundred metres I guess they can go flat out, but after that they're not good runners and then they have to give in, because either they have to run down a hole — and they usually lead you away from it and come back in a circle — or they go up a tree. When they get up the tree they pretend they're a branch and it's so easy it's not funny, poor old *bungarra*.

They dug a *bungarra* out in the winter. See in weather like this [summer] they come out. They hibernate when it's raining and they're underground for all those winter months. But on a hot day they'll come out looking for food. I was sitting watching my old uncle, old Pop really, go after a *bungarra* and he was getting close you know. He was digging must have been for two or three metres underground. But he wasn't really going straight down. It was going down and out, cos the *bungarra* was trying to dig its way out. The faster we were digging the faster this *bungarra* dug. At last Pop came to where he could see the sand getting moved. He said, 'Oh, he not far now,' and got hold of his tail and pulled him out. I tell you he was about four foot long [1.2 m], no worries. Pulled him out and knocked him on the head, cos he was still fighting but he couldn't get away. You can dig them out in the winter. They're fat as well then because they've already fattened up through summer to last through winter. That's quite often done. I saw a lot of little things done like that.

But a lot of them fellers have a good yarn with them before they kill them. They know they're going to die. There are lots of ways to talk. My old husband used to lie down next to them and that *bungarra* wouldn't move. There's another feller I knew he'd walk straight over to the sheep trough, and put one of his hands on its neck and one on its tail. He knew that the *bungarra* was there, they disappeared because of the noise coming. The *bungarra* was powerless like that. It was easy then to kill the *bungarra*. We had eleven in one day. That's one of my favourites is the *bungarra*.

The tail is the most exciting, but once when we had anthropologists with us we were very conscious of eating in front of them, two ladies. The ribs and the fat, they go well together. But you know it's really a case of not wanting to eat in front of them. They were quite happy to have a taste themselves.

I never ate bobtails but my mother did because she was at Moore River Settlement, and that's what they had there rather than *bungarras*. She used to love them. I don't think I could eat it. My grandson, one of these sou-westers showed him, went and cooked a bobtail over in Karrinyup, and he was only a little feller. When I found out that him and his cousin were eating it I said, 'What are you doing eating bobtail?' 'Oh it's good, Nanna,' he said, 'it tastes just like chicken.' Slimy, oh I couldn't believe it. Mum always ate bobtails but she came from that coastline, Dongara and Irwin River. Her father was a big man in law, old Tom my grandfather. He was one of the line cutters — that's the English word — from sacred site to sacred site, and he'd have to look after them and check the country from one point to the other.

Did I tell you about my old Dad? He used to walk along and put his hat in front of a snake. You could sort of mesmerise the snake. He'd walk away and get a little stick and come back and kill it, out of the road. There were a lot of snakes around Morawa. I knew the old people that ate carpet snake, they reckoned it was the best feed they had, better than *bungarras*. Of course when they cooked them they reckon the fat would stay in the ashes for years, it was that strong, and it was lovely. But I don't know, I never tasted it.

I've witnessed two snakes mating and you wouldn't think that — I was in a ute, me and my kids. The snakes were entwined, standing at least a metre off the ground on the very tips of their tails. They were huge snakes. I reckon they must have been six foot long [1.8 m]. And when they saw the ute well they broke apart. But the male one — it must have been the male one — charged the ute. I was driving and the faster I was reversing the faster this thing was coming. Anyway I got away from it but I was terrified, cos the cheek of this blooming snake chasing a car. I was worried about him coming up through the floorboards in the old ute cos I was only young.

I love *bardies*. I was out the bush in winter because they're easy to find. In the mulga country you get twelve, no worries, out of one tree. They'd be the best part of a foot long [0.3 m], or eight inches [20.3 cm] when they'd pick them out, even longer. They were lovely.

The quandongs* come out during the summer and spring. People make jam from them now, but those times they used to eat the seeds as well. Emus love them. They get them off the tree. I've seen white quandongs. They're real ripe when they're white. They're green and then they turn white instead of red. They reckon minerals cause it to be white, and where there's white quandongs there's minerals.

There's a little berry tree that I used to love. I still do if I can find them. They're a prickly bush. They were the same colour as the watermelon, but they also have a dainty little pink flower. You could always suck the nectar out of that. But we used to leave it because we knew that berries were going to come out, hundreds of berries and we could have a feed. The bobtails loved them. It wasn't unusual to lift the tree up and there are a couple of bobtails underneath. We weren't afraid. We were taught not to fear those things.

There are *carara** seeds and *boggada** seeds. There's a siding out from Morawa called Bowgada and I'd say that's the white man's version of *boggada*. It was just known as the *boggada* seeds. It's a curly one as a tree, *carara* tree. A prickly tree but it used to have little black and pretty gold seeds out of it, curly seeds you could eat, heaps and heaps of things. They have a station named after it cos there's that many *carara* bushes [Karara Homestead east from Perenjori on Rothsay Road]. It's always got a twist with the 'rr'. The vine would grow after cyclones. It's more or less a summer time fruit and packed out, they were just lovely. We couldn't leave them. We used to send them in on the mail truck in boxes full, go up the creek and pick them, and snotty gobbles*. There were all sorts of berries and things you could eat.

Yams you can dig and eat. Not only yams. You could dig *culyu**. That's the big purple one like a sweet potato. The leaves have a funny smell, a different smell, and you can boil them up and they say it's good for your kidneys. There's also *gumbara**. Some people call it *tumbara*. But

I think it would be more like *gumbara*. A small tomato bush, it usually grows across granites, little red tomatoes, wild tomatoes.

Those moths out of the caves, they used to throw them on the coals and they come out like *bardies*. Leave the wings you know, and that was another real good feed too. The white people call them bogongs. There's quite a bit of feed you know, the moths, bats, and small lizards and carpet snake, the *bungarra* of course.

The most beautiful orchids you could ever see used to grow in Morawa, Rabbit Orchids, Spider Orchids, Donkey Orchids, dozens of these standing up like kings and queens you know, so pretty, all these beautiful flowers. Every spring, end of winter they'd be there in hundreds, only a short time during the winter and just after spring would come on, but they die easily. You wouldn't find one now, just all gone. People (tourists) go and look for the wildflowers, everlastings and star flowers and those sorts of things, they're everywhere. They last a long time but not those orchids. They can never be replaced. They're talking about some place down here where there's orchid farming that was really beautiful. You'd find one little Rabbit Orchid and then all of a sudden it's like they were a family growing. It looked like a rabbit's head with two ears, a green thing. Somebody spotted them somewhere and I saw the photo in the paper and I thought, 'God, how lucky we were to see them growing everywhere.' But of course they've been taken out.

Healing and bush medicine

I have a bottle of bush medicine. Some time ago I used to have terrible bad kidneys, and I went up to Mount Magnet and out from there there's a little bush. My sister-in-law at the time had cancer on her thigh. It kept growing to the size of a small football, a kid's football, and they kept taking it out. Then there was a big thing going on in Perth, Aboriginal arts and that and I was here, and I saw her walking with a walking stick, she came from Queensland. So I said, 'Oh gee, is there any chance that you'd want to try this Yamatji medicine, if I gave you some?' 'Oh,' she said, 'I'll try anything. Because,' she said, 'they're going to take my leg off if I don't. And,' she said, 'I'm just trying to last out some studies before they do that.'

So I brought a flagon in the next day, a big bottle, and I said, 'You drink that any time you want to.' I had another one. I never had kidney complaints for years after. That's what I had it for. But her, inside three weeks the cancer had stopped growing, and six weeks after she rang me up and she was laughing. She said the doctor said to her, 'There's only a scar there. It must have been the treatment you had.' But she didn't have any treatment, and she remarked then, 'Well you and I know better than that don't we?' She hasn't had the cancer return either, and that's a good thirty or twenty-five years now.

I don't know what the whitefeller's name is, but we just knew the medicine bush and mixed it up. There's so much in the bush that comes from the ground that can cure things like cancer and other things. There's internal medicine, there's one that we brew up, and there's another one. My brother's kids had scabies. You know they were going through all the country towns and he was living in Morawa and he had three little boys. They had these sores all over them, head, backside, legs, ankles, hands, fingers, arms, everywhere. So we went out in the bush and got this bush flower. It was a real waxy one with a pretty purple flower. I can't tell you the name, I'd have to show you. But you dry it out and you boil it up in a billy can and add it to the bath water. Those kids never had scabies after that. It was for your skin, like a cure.

From different areas people had different medicines. Like I said, there must be hundreds of thousands of cures the Aboriginals are familiar with. I know it's true because I've seen the proof that it works, and nobody can dispute it. It isn't only for Aboriginals because I gave a shopkeeper some too. She had cancer on the knee. It just left a big scar. And there's so many different species that all look alike of these bushes.

I've been drinking that medicine, it's bitter as gall. I've had this thing in my throat. I mean it isn't malignant, I've had it tested. It stopped me from breathing properly, but I've got around that. Seems all right. I had my daughter with me when I went and got that medicine bush. I've been making it all the time. My daughter has too, and son. Because it's my way of thinking that while the sap is still in that bark it's more valuable. But they did say, or I was told, that you could boil the roots and they were quite good. They were the best they reckon, they were the strongest, but I don't see it like that. I see this plant itself sapping up the minerals in the ground, and the minerals is the important part to Aboriginal survival. That's the way I see it.

There are quite a few white success stories on that home medicine too. A lot. But they don't tell anybody anything or where they get it. Other people exploit it. They were down here selling it at a market somewhere for three hundred dollars a flagon. I only just heard of it the other day. Another woman was selling it for a hundred dollars a bottle, using it as a money-making thing. Well it will never be a success, because it was never meant to do that. There's old spirits out there that wouldn't like that at all. They just wouldn't like it. I don't sell it and I don't exploit it, but I know it's good. I've got a sick daughter. I've got no doubt it will cure her, for a long, long time once that stuff gets in her body. I don't like to tell anyone. What I see in telling people where it come from and how, it's like a prostitution of the Aboriginal culture.

Minerals

An old friend came along one day and asked my husband to come out and look at what he'd found. He said, 'I'm sure it's emerald.' I don't know whether emeralds are found in those areas or what, but these were the prettiest green stone crystals. But my husband was never a man to want to profit out of anything, even gold. Some people said, 'Do something for us.' *Kooda** they called him. He said, 'Oh I'll find out about it. Let's go and look for the gold.' But he never ever did. It didn't matter to him. He was never interested in profit, 'I'll work for my money.' He didn't want to become rich. He just wanted to be himself. It was pretty good thinking.

They took us to this other place and there was copper in the bottom, but all through that copper was gold. It was a mine somebody started years before. All through that place was copper. Sounds like its left on the hill you know but it's not. Somebody went and dug it out again and had a look. In the bottom of that thing it was brown, and round the edges where this copper started was all green. You just knew it was copper, and there was gold running through the copper. I don't know whether they pegged it or not.

I went back there after and had a look to see if it was still there and it had all caved in. We dug around a bit, but there was some sort of lizard, quite big, about two feet long, shiny black and white banded. They moved very fast and I immediately reckoned they were vicious and if they bit you you'd probably get poisoned. I've seen them only in that country when you dig down. You don't see them skipping along the road or crossroads. They live underground mostly.

Lennie used to be a blooming front-end loader driver, loading up trucks with gold and gravel. Well they were all going along the streets of Mount Magnet picking up pieces of gold. The rumours were flying around, 'Where did Lennie get the gold? Where did he get the gravel?' I said, 'Oh don't ask me.' I didn't worry about telling them nothing, but there were no seams of gold there anyway. It was there somewhere but they didn't pick any big pieces of gold up. But the gold was there and may be still there. It was quite funny. They were running along the street picking up bits of gold. In those days it was only thirty-three pounds an ounce. They might have sort of gone out and got tins full of it in Yalgoo and Magnet, mostly in Yalgoo, and sell it to a certain person. I suppose he ordered up and sold it in drums. They get their money's worth just from a powdered milk tin full. It was what they never had, money, to buy.

My mother used to live on the Coalseam. That was within the tribe, the Coalseam. I've got a story that Norm Harris wrote up and it quite often mentions the Coalseam, cos he went to that Coalseam with my mother, to stay with her on the holidays. It's all documented before he died and it wasn't to be released until he died, he said, because some people mightn't like what he wrote.

I met an old chap from the university in Adelaide and he said he used to work for the Melbourne Museum and they went on an expedition. They took this old Aboriginal feller and different other ones, and they found caves that were thirty and forty foot [9.1 m and 12.2 m] high, with paintings on the ceiling and everywhere, on the way up to central Australia. Just unbelievable. They asked this one old feller to show them the centre of Australia and when they were just about there they said, 'Can you tell us where the centre is?' He said, 'Oh yeah no worries.' He grabbed a little stick and he put it in the ground and he said, 'That's the middle.' They brought out all their equipment and it was spot on, the dead centre. These fellers that told me these things said that seeing is believing. How could any blackfeller or any man get up on that wall to do a painting on the ceiling of a cave? They said it must have meant that they had something to help them get up there. But I don't believe that. I reckon the cave floor had been dug out.

That chap was an old whitefeller that came over to an exhibition that Mick Little put on in '86 or '87, and he was telling me about that old bloke and gave me his book. When he was there at that spot in the centre he grabbed a piece of slate and cleaned it up — it was about A4 size — and painted on it. It wasn't much painting to do, but he painted a cattle skull in the dirt and a little stick next to it and a dry tree. He said, 'I've waited for years to give it to somebody and I've found the right person.' It was me, and I said, 'Oh no, I couldn't take it.' 'No no,' he said, 'you are the right person. I know you are.' He was an old whitefeller. He must be dead now. He'd been through a heck of a lot. When we went over there with that exhibition of Mick's he never left us. Every day he'd sit and he'd listen to us talk about the paintings and what they meant. He was just unbelievable. I can't remember his blooming name now, that's '86 or '87 we were over there, just after the America's Cup.

Ochre

Aboriginal people walked from Queensland to Cue. There's Wilgi Mia they call it. There's no red ochre in Queensland and that's a fact. I read it in an archaeologist's book that Greg had in Adelaide. But they knew exactly where to walk. They used to come all that way to get that red ochre and walk back. They use it in the ceremonies.

On the top of a hill at another place there was all this white ochre. The goats would run up and down that much they left a hole in the top of the hill like a volcano. The white ochre was all powdered up on the top. The kids used to go up and get a bucket of this white ochre and they'd bring it back, but I haven't had any since and it's worn away something bad. It was huge, just unbelievable. I saw it forty years before. It was funny. Now it's worn, worn, worn. I go up there all the time. One old feller said, 'I seen you there before. You was only a little girl.' I said, 'I never saw it till I was a woman.' And he said, 'That's your first life I'm talking about.' He said, 'That's why you go back there all the time.' Oh God, where am I coming from? But I do believe in reincarnation. That's one thing I do believe.

Barnong Station, that's where that ochre is, and on Karara there's other pieces. It's already been registered before. It's quite flat ground and then a huge hole in the ground fifteen foot [4.6 m] deep. How Aboriginal people ever got in there and mined that ochre one would never know. My guess is they put a stick down or bit of a tree and climbed up and down it. They were not fifteen foot tall surely. They had to have something like a tree. Everybody knows about it. It's just like a hole in the ground. You walk and fall straight down.

Some of our ancestors' tools are there too. We were advised that we should be able to take those artefacts before they're destroyed by somebody else taking them away. There are tools like club sort of things, probably for powdering the ochre up, and we found another one at another place, a real club-like thing, but the boys just left it. When we went back to get it, it was gone. Somebody else must have picked it up. They've done that all through that country. Twenty years ago there was a big argument. Some blokes went out there, went into a cave and found all these stones, stones I know connected with the law. Someone complained to the authorities about it and they were supposed to give them back. I don't really know whether they gave them back or put them back, but a nephew of mine reckons he knows where they are. The Teaching Stones they call them. I don't know whether they're still there or not.

6.
Dreaming stories

The law was very strict and we were not allowed to talk while elders were talking, or to be seen to be rowdy or interfere with conversations, because the law says that uncles don't talk to nieces. You weren't supposed to have anything to do with your uncles, very harsh I suppose. But we did talk to our uncles, and one in particular had been through the law, Uncle Tom [mother's brother]. He used to tell us little stories about the bush in the Dreamtime that we had no idea about, but it was fascinating and I always listened. Uncle Tom was one of the great family storytellers, along with my mother and my Aunty Eva. They told us whatever they had on their minds. It was a passed on thing but we weren't to know that. We were fascinated by the stories. We used to lie out in the open on hot nights, and you got the hot wind and all that, snakes all night. It was part of our life.

Besides what my Mum told me, and uncle and other old people, my aunty really told me a lot. But there were a lot of things she wasn't allowed to talk about, mainly because I think they were men's business or part of the business. But my Mum went through the law, so I was told, out from Mullewa, and the last of the law went on to Pia Station. There are two Pias. There's Pia One and Pia Two, and one goes not far out [from Mullewa] and the other one is further, north-east, that one's run by the Simpsons. Might be P-y-a but I don't think so. It's P-i-a.

The **djurrnda** stone

Really and truly I couldn't fault my mother, the stories she told to me. I know where there's women's business and other big corroboree grounds, and hidden things in different places. My mother told me about them and about one place in particular that's to do with fresh water in a big lake. She told me about a big stone in a lake east of Morawa — it's now known as Lake Moore, and it's on the other side of Mount Gibson. It's shaped like a mushroom, that's what we were told anyway. Only special people would ever see the stone, and there's a special time of the year it would rise out of the lake. So, fair enough. I laughed because that was the story. *Djurrnda** stone they called it, with that twist to the 'r', *djurrnda*.

Old Norm and Aunty Eva went out many times to find it, because the word was it was pure gold and they wanted to see if it was true, but they went looking north. They hunted and hunted but this stone's supposed to be is Lake Moore, and Lake Monger was where they were going all the time. Mount Gibson is in between these two lakes. So Lake Moore is the one that's got this fresh water. I nearly freaked out knowing all these things. Many people say there was fresh water in the middle of Lake Moore, and all around the side there was fresh water. At one time there must have been freshwater lakes or something, an underground river maybe.

The mushroom stone came out through archaeologists' studies. And there are artefacts that match the stones. You know just pushed up through the ground. It's a permanent thing. When I met this chap that worked down there, something to do with tourism, he showed me a map that showed everything my mother said, including the story about the *djurrnda* stone. That's east of where we were but it's still in Widi country. It's just so uncanny really that my mother told me years ago about the *djurrnda* stone. I've never set eyes on any of it. We didn't have an opportunity. We had no vehicles and you know we weren't actually taken on walkabouts like normal tribal people. We were half civilised.

There's a little bit more to it. I didn't tell you the whole truth of those golden mushrooms. I went up to Paynes Find and somehow through the night I had some sort of vision or dream. This person was telling me about this stone. It wasn't really a golden mushroom like the one in the lake could have been. It was more to the point of some small tribe getting killed by mushrooms. I've only just had this story. Where it came from goodness knows. All these little mushrooms can be found, the mushroom stones. They've turned to stone. I could see them in my dream. Strange isn't it? It came to me the other day. I quite often get stories.

One feller I know used to work on a station that joins Mount Gibson, and you know how station owners have their paddocks mapped out?

The sheep were all disappearing. You know, he had to go round up the sheep and he'd do it on motorbike and horseback. But he said they ran into these sheep that were just heavily laden with wool and hadn't been shorn, which they call stragglers. They had inches and inches of wool, to the point where they could barely walk. So they followed them to this place, and then all of a sudden the ground dropped, more like I suppose crater-like, and they were wondering where this water was coming from to feed these sheep, cos their pads were going up this little hill in the middle of the crater and the water was running uphill. The water was in the top of this hill. It was being pushed up somehow. I was told that before by other people.

The map also gives a list of the animals that were there, and in that list is *dunart*. When I was telling the anthro he said, 'Oh, well, I'm sure this must be the story you told me about the Dunart and the Bungarra.' This is the country, so I'm sure it is too. I've never heard anybody else tell the story about the *dunart* but that's what that little animal was. That's also in the list, the mushroom stone, and some other animals that are found down here, some possums and bilby. I think originally they wanted to make a tourist thing of it and so somebody went out there and listed all the animals and all the birds and everything. But I don't think it ever got off the ground. Too rough the country. Anyway all those things my mother was telling me about, I never knew whether they were true or not because I couldn't prove it.

The Dreaming, the spiritual things that are just unreal, made the people out of the animals. It's unreal and yet it's understandable; creation days the old people told us. Most of us now are young compared to those people. That's really because all the creatures, the birds, animals, all of them became Aboriginals, and through punishment or whatever that's how they come about. Funniest thing. Every being has a spirit behind it. Everybody has their different spirit [totem]. It could be an animal like a bird or a snake.

Beemarra

In that area I mentioned (above) there is a Dreaming track. You know how they say God is everywhere. This Beemarra would have been similar to the white man's God, because he's everywhere. They come from over there, Ernabella and into Western Australia, called Yakabindie in Western Australia but east, out from Wiluna, and there were two males and two female snakes. But I wouldn't go into that story.

The snakes separated and each one took a different direction. One went up north, right up to the Kimberleys. One went down over here to Wongi land and from there it travelled on. I don't know where ours went but I think it was Yakabindie. Our Dreaming track comes from Yakabindie to Cue and Lake Darlot. It covers the Mount Gibson area and the two lakes, and right away to near Northampton and the Bowes River, and down along the coast. Even the Wadjari people call that the Beemarra. I don't know whether it was before white settlement, but it must have been. They separated to the north and to the Midwest and lived in the south and the midsouth around Pingelly to populate and give water. They created the water and the land. This story comes from the Dreaming. This is before people.

It's fascinating and it conflicts with Christianity in one way, and yet it's quite like Christianity. I mean in death they buried people in the white words, 'ashes to ashes and dust to dust.' But our way, we return to the lands and the ground we came from. Even in the Bible it says God took a handful of sand and made man, and we came from the ground.

Christianity is a white man's name for believing in a saviour, but God says in the Bible, 'Believe in me for I am the truth,' and that's what I say is God. You can't put a face on God, but you can put a face on that Beemarra. And I always ask the question, on what day did God create water? I keep coming back to it. I can't help asking the question, but they didn't bring that water, it was here all the time. In the Aboriginal Dreaming, Beemarra created the water. What I'm saying is the white people brought Christianity to the Aboriginal people. They didn't bring the water. The water was there all the time because Beemarra created the water. Aboriginal names for Beemarra are slightly different between different areas. In some places they call it the Rainbow Snake and other places they call him Wagyl.

Red kangaroo

There's another place up there in Cue. Right next to Cue is Widi country and then it goes east, and there's a place called Wilgi Mia that every man and his dog knows about. People came from Queensland for that red *wilgi*, red ochre. There was a big red kangaroo and he was eating all the food and chasing all the other kangaroos out, the *marrloo* and *bigudas*, rock kangaroos. He kept chasing them out and the Aboriginals there were starting to get hungry because this big boomer was eating everything. So they all got together and they started throwing magic at it, but that didn't work on the kangaroo and he still ran rampant. So all the tribes from all around got together with their spears and boomerangs. They chased him down to this big hill and they hit him with everything. Of course they killed him, he rolled down that hill and landed with a crash and made a big hole. The red ochre is the blood of that red kangaroo. It's a sacred stone of course. That's what happened and they said because he was so big that was why it was such a big minefield for red ochre.

Porcupine (echidna)

The Porcupine was a greedy, greedy frog. Well he was like a frog and he was water. There was a drought during the summer and the water was drying up. But there was one place where there was plenty of water, so they used to go there and get their water and keep it safe, and nobody was greedy. But the frog went along and he drank all the water. While he was drinking the water all the other Aboriginals got on the hill and they threw spears at him. So he had to carry all those spears. That's how he got his spears (quills), cos he was greedy and drank all the water.

Bungarra and Emu

There's a story about the Bungarra and the Emu. Well Emu has always been an arrogant sticky-beak who picks up everything and is jealous too, but he was also friendly. But he got jealous of the Bungarra because they called it a racehorse goanna — you know, eventually the whitefellers did cos it could run. So he said, 'All right Bungarra, me and you have a race,' he said in their own lingo. Somebody kicked them off, I think it was the Turtle, and away they went. Well the Bungarra, he could run, but he had only little short legs. So of course Emu started out and beat him. So the poor little Bungarra he came back and he was blowing and going on and the Emu was giving him cheek. Oh, you know, things like 'You can't run.' And Bungarra sat and he thought. He said, 'All right then, I'll give you another race. I bet I can beat you in a race around that tree.' And the Emu said, 'Oh no worries.' So they got on their marks again and they went round the tree. Well the Bungarra ran straight onto the tree trunk, and ran it. He won the race cos the Emu couldn't turn quickly. So that's how the Bungarra beat him in the race. Emu says, 'Oh no worries,' but that's just our way of telling the story to kids. Storytelling to kids and that, that's the sort of lingo they'd understand.

Emu and Turkey

There was another story about the Emu and the Turkey and why the turkey lays only two eggs. The emu features a lot in that area and I just sometimes wonder why, and the black *bungarra*. The Emu was always a show off. The Turkey was smaller and Emu used to be the big boss, it could fly and the Turkey could fly too. But the Emu being a standover he was always hard on Turkey. One day the Emu went and smashed all of Turkey's eggs, except two. That's why the turkey has only one partner and they can only lay two eggs. So when Turkey found out, oh he was really crying and going on, you know hurt and he wanted to get this Emu back. So he tucked his wings up under him and he said, 'Oh look here Emu. I shortened my wings.' And because the Emu never wanted Turkey to beat him he said, 'Oh well, you can take mine off too.' So the Turkey said, 'Yeah I will.' So he burnt the wings off the Emu, from the elbows. And when it all died down he only had half of them, little tiny wings both sides. Emu thought he was clever but when he went to fly he couldn't, and the Turkey jumped up and flew, and he went away laughing at the Emu. But you see that's why the turkey lays only two eggs. The emu lays heaps of eggs. But the turkey can fly, and the emu can't.

Bungarra and Dunart

They had all sorts of stories attached to the Bungarra. I don't know whether I told you about how he got his colours. Well then, him and that Dunart — cos this story comes from up our way — they were very good friends. But the Bungarra was a bit of a standover. The little Dunart — the little kangaroo mouse — he hopped along listening to all this — go an' get this, go and fetch that. Anyhow, one day they happened to crawl over some yellow ochre. When the Bungarra looked down — cos he was naturally grey – he said, 'Oh that's a pretty yellow colour. Can you paint me?' The little Dunart, little feller said, 'Oh yeah, I'll do it.' But he was so little you know and he got tired.

   He started off in good fashion. He was doing his little circles and lines across the Bungarra. But he took a long time and the Bungarra looked over his shoulder and he got wild you know, 'Come on, hurry up. You're making a mess of me!' Anyway the little Dunart he made big long strokes along the tail so he had the colours all in line, a few dots here and there. The Bungarra looked again and he said, 'You made me ugly didn't you?' He elbowed him right in the middle of the chest, and the poor little Dunart, he fell over on his back and his breast bone jumped straight out and he was lying on his back like a turtle. The Bungarra was cursing him and going on and he said he was ugly, and the little Dunart was lying there trying to get up. But it tells that story of how the *bungarra* got the colours and the *dunart* got the permanent lump in its breast.

The Dunart's a little kangaroo mouse. It's really small. But they eat everything, chop chop chop chop chop. We heard those stories about the Bungarra when I was a little kid, and the Dunart, and I never knew quite anything about the *dunart*, except that it was like a field mouse and it feeds its young through a pouch like a kangaroo. So we just call it a kangaroo mouse, but it was a *dunart*.

I picked up the paper a couple of weeks ago and I looked where they had some pictures of a *dunart*. I've told you the story about the Dunart. But when I saw that little face in the picture it was quite funny. Because they reckon when they get going to have a feed — and I guess these fellers with their infrared cameras or whatever it is watch them you know — they have these teeth come out and they yak-yak-yak-yak-yak, and eat. It was quite funny too. Errol, my eldest son, of course he found tracks and he said, 'Mum, there's heaps of little tracks here,' not far from the Mount Gibson gate. I said, 'What do they look like?' He said, 'They're little kangaroo tracks.' 'Oh,' I said, 'I know what they are.' 'What?' I said, *'Dunart*. They got a little track like a kangaroo, same kind of foot.' Ron [Parker] had a look and he said, 'Oh I dunno what they are,' but that's what they are. They've shifted out since the mining began.

Sturt pea

There's another story about the Sturt Pea. Our Dreaming track of course goes right across, a little bit south-east. But the story's there in the desert when the young man and a woman they got together, and they shouldn't have married you know. It was the wrong skin. So they ran away and of course they were getting chased and followed by *moban** people who were working magic and trying to send them off. But they managed to stay clear of all that and they ran ran ran. But at last they ran out of water. So he got her to suck on this little pebble. He said, 'If you get thirsty just keep on sucking on this pebble, and I'll go back and try and find water for us.' It worked for a while but wouldn't do for long.

So he left her, but when he got back to his tribe he was punished and he couldn't go back for her. Then some months later he went back there and all he found were pretty red flowers that were branching out everywhere. The rain had washed the seeds out and they were flowing, and those seeds were really the stones that came from that woman. They went into her stomach I guess. So that's how they come about. When the rain came it would carry those stones [seeds] everywhere and they branched out and grew in the desert.

The Man in the Moon and the Sun Woman

The Sun Woman was one of the best runners in the tribe. And when the hunters used to go away from the tribe, other tribesmen would come and they'd try to steal the wives. But then this one old feller discovered how to make a fire. So the other tribesmen came to try to steal that. They were sneaking around trying to find the coal, so the old feller gave it to the fastest runner, the Sun Woman, and she ran away with it as fast as she could. She ran so fast that she ran right up into the air, and as she ran that coal was getting brighter and brighter. She was wheeling it and she ended up rolling it around the earth. That's how they created night and day. Running behind her was always the Man in the Moon, because he was chasing her for his wife and he got caught in this — round and round — so he ended up in the moon. That's how the Man in the Moon and day and night came about.

The Man in the Moon was locked up there and somebody else wanted to fight him. He was probably jealous of him being in the moon and chasing the Sun Woman. Jealousy came into it a lot. And every time he hit that moon a big chunk of it would fall out, creating the meteorites and all the dark colours of the moon, and sparks would fly off every time he hit him and they turned into the stars.

Bossy Snake

Did I tell you about the big black Snake? A big Aboriginal feller tracked it. He wanted to kill it because it was, you know, a bossy thing. Well he followed it all over the country because it was a bad snake. He followed it towards Karara Station, followed it all around there, fighting with it until he caught it at Karara Station, further up in the granites. The top of the granites — now low-lying granites — look like a snake's track. The first impression you get just looking from the road, you're looking straight up the top of the granites and you can see the snake wriggling on top and there are no stones there. All the stones are at the bottom of the granite on each side. That's where they had the fight and they rocked all that granite. But the Snake got away. Everybody believes that that Snake is still there. They reckon he still roams around there, this Dreamtime Snake. He was not the Beemarra, can't be. But he's a big black snake that you got to be careful of they reckon.

Two men and a woman

There were two men and a woman that followed two *bungarras*. They wanted to kill these *bungarras* and they travelled for miles. Occasionally they saw the *bungarras* ahead of them. Then they got to this place — it's not far from Morawa, out bush. The *bungarra* said, 'Oh they're getting too close so we'll have to trick them.' One *bungarra* got on the back of the other so that the Aboriginals thought they had separated. But when the bungarras got to this place somebody killed them. In one place there's this huge hill further away, separated. It's a granite and one's an ochre place where the two stones are standing waiting for the woman to come. It shows where the two men are still there in stone, waiting for the woman to come back. The woman had walked off and left them cos she was still chasing these *bungarras*. They're still there, wearing away a bit though. Further away in this other place, there's this granite where there's the outline in stone of a *bungarra* standing, and there's all these things [plates of stone] around it, and another *bungarra*'s head. That's what all those plates look like; it's like a teaching place or something. It's two stones but to us Aboriginal people when you look at it you would say it's a Lizard Dreaming place or Bungarra Dreaming.

I'm talking about two different places but that's how they came about. That's what they look like to me, and there are several different places I've run into like that as well. The plates of stone obviously come out of the ground somewhere. They're little square things like you've got an altar or a schoolroom. You can liken it to anything where you've been, but it's strange that it's sitting up in the middle of the bush. It's like an altar on the side of this hill. It's uncanny, the shape of the animal. The *bungarra* is on the side of that hill still today. I took photos of it. It's just so unbelievable, all these flats of stone on the side of the granite, a little church-like thing. It's really hard to describe and yet it isn't because you can see it in your mind. And all over the place, all over that hill were lizard traps. They must have feasted on these lizards. Cos the *bungarras* eat lizards too. You know, pig eat pig and chook eat chook and all that sort of thing, white meat. That's how *bungarras* are. Not all people eat them.

Crocodile and Beemarra

I was surprised because there was one story this chap was telling down in Fremantle about the Crocodile that went down there and had a fight with the Shark. I said, 'Well, I would never have connected a crocodile with them, coming this far down.' It was a funny thing cos an anthropologist said, 'oh it's a very funny thing' he said, 'because I never would believe that, That Crocodile fighting track is all the way up the north coast.' Well Crocodile fought with the Shark but came off badly and couldn't travel back to the Kimberley, so he came up at the mouth of the Murchison River at Kalbarri, and that story was told there, then he tried to run off and there's supposed to be a tributary that he couldn't get out of. So he turned around and he went out to find another escape and the Beemarra (this is the Wagyl down here) told him to go to Yanchep [north of Perth] to hide and that's where some big rocks were formed as part of its tail you know.

There are so many other stories and I know now what they're called. I saw it somewhere in the Centre, in different tribal areas and I know where it is. It's so uncanny I can't believe it. It just dropped in my lap, just put it that way. I'd get these messages. I was telling you about this one bloke, his grandfather was born up there. He was up there working and told us a story about the golden mushrooms. Of course the golden mushroom is a myth sort of thing. Nobody's seen it. Only special people will ever see that. There are lots more stories and I just can't put them all at once. That's why you've always got to come back and I remember another one.

7.
Spirit life

My sister Gloria in Dalwallinu was quite simply tormented, and her kids and grandchildren were terrified. They were talking in their dreams to spirits that weren't there. And they were getting weird dreams that there was blood everywhere, and this man running with a skin on him and carrying a spear, and there were people lying dead everywhere. There must have been a massacre there at some time. Different people within the family were getting contacted by these spirits. The dreams were all similar. So I took a friend of mine, he's a *moban* man, to that place and they have never had the problem since.

After we went to Dalwallinu and all came away, he rang me up and he said, 'Did they ever have a lot of rain there?' I said, 'Oh not as far as I know.' During the drought there was no rain. It was like every other place in Western Australia. But he said, 'That man was wearing the skin of a rainmaker. Kangaroo running.' From that time to now my sister has never had that problem. He contacted them through mental telepathy I guess you'd call it, contacted the spirits themselves. Well they have all sorts of power. I've seen it happen so I can't disbelieve it.

That time, one of the little girls was playing in the park and she was sitting on one swing, and the other swing was swinging and she's talking. So the mother said, 'What are you talking about? Who are you talking to?' 'My friend, can't you see my friend?' It was a spirit I think. And she'd be sharing out her lollies, 'One for you and one for me.' She was carrying on conversations and all with this little friend. I mean that's not unusual. A lot of kids do that when they play on their own a lot. It's not unusual anywhere. But at that time Gloria and her granddaughter were getting troubled by these older people, having the same dream about blood and being chased.

7. Spirit life

It was the same people and the same incident. That was going on through the kids and everything, the same family. Anyway what come out of it was the *moban* man said there was a spirit trying to contact somebody and tell them about the massacre that went on there. Also there was a house fire and one little girl got burnt in the house fire and the mother was looking for her spirit, or something to that effect, and she — they don't quite know what the mother was screaming. Strangely enough, one of the kids drew a picture of it. That's what happened. That old rainmaker with a kangaroo skin on was trying to tell somebody about the massacre and why there was no rain I guess, and the problems they had. A lot of people died at that massacre. The only way to find out if it ever happened would be to check in the archives. It may have been documented somewhere, but I doubt it. But it was settled when the *moban* man went there, and that was good because he'd been given that power.

There's lots of things in Dalwallinu. I mean it's a strange town. A lot of the land was cleared and they usually pile up all these rocks. Those rocks could tell a lot, there's a lot of stories in the granites and caves in that area. There are a lot of things there. It's really for these people with the Noongar claim and the Noongar blood to go through and look at. It's part of ours as well, but I cut the bottom part off in the claim. It was documented through Tindale that that area was Widi country. I think people who use that thing as their data, they've got a tribal boundary going straight down the railway line, and that's not true. That railway line came hundreds of years later. You know the way those people all mixed and communicated was through their language. There was no language barrier. Tindale wrote in his letter that another tribe called Ballardong came from Northam. I never stayed in Dalwallinu, ever. I've been through and around there and looked around, sticky-beaked around, but I don't like the country. Got to be country that I like before I look in.

If you go from here to Bindoon and further, Walebing or right across to Dalwallinu, you'll see piles of sand, stones and little granite outcrops on land. I can't help but wonder every time I pass what sacred site was there and what they destroyed. Because if you were to go all through those piles of stones and things, the whole place is scattered with artefacts and creeks and rivers and little things like that, that if people were to study they'd find out a lot more about what's there. My old Dad used to do stone picking, had to pick up all the stones out of the paddock to clear the land so they could put crops in. This was in Morawa all around, all the farming. I saw it on the way to Dalwallinu.

I was driving between Morawa and Mingenew. It's beautiful country with all the wild flowers. I heard a man crying at one spot, the spirit of my old grandfather who died on the roads. The second time I heard women crying, wailing. I have spiritual contact with those people. A lot of places I go I'm guided by the spirits. It's hard to understand.

I always used to have this dream when I was small, and it followed me right through till I was well into my thirties, that I was standing under the sea on a reef. I was in this bluish kind of dress and the water was gushing in you know, roaring, but it never harmed me. It'd repeat and I'd have it again in a couple of months. In the end cos I wasn't scared, I think maybe it was my first life. I was only about eight or ten years old. That dream repeated on me for thirty years and then it went because I started to ignore it. But somehow to me it was telling me something. I do believe in reincarnation because I've often had similar dreams.

Other things that happened — well my brother Bill discovered this ochre, and it's the prettiest ochre. You know, during the rain it washes it clean and you see it all running off the hill. I went there about thirty-five years ago. That's the last time I went there, before I was taken on site clearances. When I went there — I must have been in my thirties — to see the place when Bill was showing us. I used to go back there to that same place every time I went to Morawa. Every time I went past I'd go in. I was up there a couple of weeks ago and nobody goes there, I didn't see any tracks. The road is like a gully. It's all washed out and it's hard to get into. You could get in with a car and that's what we did do. Of course you need a four-wheel drive. There's not too many sheep there now — the drought no doubt — and there was a lot of land.

Something kept taking me back to that place. I wanted to find something, and this feller told me then that it was something like a reincarnation of me. I had to keep going back to this place, to a previous life. I'd go back and I'd go back and I go back, but I haven't been there lately cos I'd start to get a bit worried about it, me wanting to go there all the time. Anyway it's very hard to get there, very rough. The hill itself was really high. It was a big white hill, apart from the other parts you know, the other colours. I was told by other Aboriginal people that it was my place, and somebody had seen me there before as a little girl.

Every colour of ochre you can find is there and I'd say that it would be a big sacred site because ochre's scarce, it's not everywhere. And where they find red ochre they find iron ore, because iron ore's compressed red ochre. A geologist was telling me they don't want to see the other colours.

Different other times you know people get those messages. My brother [Bill] used to have a dream about this big black snake that goes all over that country. People have tried to kill it. He's a bad snake, that bossy Snake I was telling you about before. My brother's seen it at a place where there's ochre and he said he'd never seen such a big snake before in his life. He was warden for plants and all that then. It wasn't CALM [the former WA Department of Conservation and Land Management]. It's before CALM was invented I think. Flowers and fauna and wildlife whatever it was. It was a different name anyway. He said everywhere he went there was this big black snake.

He went up to Broome for a few years and while he was there he used to feed this big black snake. He'd go away into town and he'd come back. They let him stay at this place to look after it. They used to bring his food out and everything just to mind the place and he'd go into town every now and then. But when he came back he'd walk around the camp and see where that snake's been for a feed and that, scraps and whatever, nothing in particular. What leftovers he had, fish usually. Because he was up there on the coast and he used to go fishing for the mud crabs and all that. He was on his own there. All he had to do was talk to the snake. Bit lonely where he was, but anyway. Different other times he saw it. But he reckoned each place he went to that big snake comes up. Well, why would that be? I can't understand. Never harms him. It just shows itself. Actually when I was speaking to him last he wanted to go bush again.

My brother Bill died on 10 August 2007, and he was buried two weeks after in Morawa. That could have been our family totem because he was the eldest in the family, but I don't know. At his funeral later on in the night, they opened all the doors in the hotel and told them to help themselves and there was free food. I was so shocked. Some of the young fellers were starving hungry and when I told them they couldn't believe it. They were too frightened to go, but others went and had a feed.

But I tell you I see figures, somebody walking around every now and then. Sometimes it's a girl but sometimes it's a man. I went to my niece's once and she told me, 'Oh Aunty,' she said, 'did you notice anything funny about the sister?' We call her Ninny. That's Gloria's daughter. It's short for Linley. I said, 'Yes, she never spoke to me.' 'Yeah, you know why?' she said, 'She was shaking.' I said, 'Why?' 'Well,' she said, 'as you pulled up she saw this man standing over the other side of the car and he had a blue shirt on. But he wasn't there.' So she rushed inside and she was shaking nearly crying.

She didn't know how to tell me about this man standing there and I said to her, 'It's my old brother,' because he always was close to me and I've got that feeling all the time he's somewhere there and I miss him heaps. Me and my brother were very close and we lived our teenage years in Morawa. When I came down here to school, he and I came down we were put in hostels and he didn't like the place. So his stay was short-lived you know. Eight or nine months and he left, and I stayed eighteen months and that was too much, so I took off back home to Morawa. Went to my mother, but there was no high school so I had to go to Mullewa. My brother paid for my board and lodging and all that so I could go to school. He was only getting four pounds a week, but he'd pay two pounds every fortnight for my board from my aunties.

He was only five years older than me, but he and I lived most of our young lives together before we got married. He lived there in Morawa after he married. But when I got married of course I went to my husband's country up there in Mount Magnet. But like I must have told you over and over I used to travel all over that bush.

Talking to animals

You can talk to animals. Birds. There's a big connection. Another friend of mine, we went out to this animal park at Caversham. There were four dingoes in a little tiny cage. I don't think it would have been as big as this cage here [fenced-in area for workmen]. When they saw us come there well they rushed to the fence, and you could see it in their eyes that they wanted to talk or wanted something. So he sat down and he was talking to them in *lingo*, and then he said, 'I got to go now mate.' They just howled. They howled so loud the zookeeper in Caversham ran up. Well I ran too, I took off. I didn't want them to think we were tormenting the animals. 'What happened to them, what happened?' I couldn't go any faster so I said, 'Oh, they just started howling when we walked away.'

But that connection was definitely there. He was saying things like, 'You want to get out poor old feller? You want to go home don't you? What if I let you out?' and things like that. And they were sitting there, all four of them, heads down looking into his eyes. I couldn't get over it. If I had had a movie camera I would have taken it, cos it was so plain.

There is a connection I've got no doubt. I've seen my husband Lennie Martin do something similar. Me and him and the kids went along one day just out the bush for a ride, it was hot day and there was this *bungarra* under a tree. I was saying, 'Grab that *bungarra* quickly, take it home and cook it.' He said, 'Oh, you don't want to do that.' 'Yes I do.' The kids too. The kids were quiet watching. He went along to the tree where the thing was, and he lay down on his side and he talked to him. But he let him go and he got up and walked away. He said, 'I can't kill him.'

You can talk to crows and magpies. Always they bring you bad news or good news, but mostly bad news. The best way is to feed them, but they get very demanding. A friend of mine used to feed them and he went away. I used to paint you know. This bird came along and I was sitting in the sunshine, wintertime it was, and he came and he sat on the tree. He was there, cark cark cark away. And then he came and he flew past, put his shadow on the painting. He sat on the connection, you know where the electricity connects to the house, sitting there shouting like a maniac. So I had to get up and chuck a piece of bread out for him. He was fine then. They know exactly what they're doing the crows, and the magpies. They knew I was painting and that was a way of making me take notice. A magpie did that the same way. I was painting out in the back and you wouldn't believe what he did. He made that much noise and I ignored him because I wanted to get this painting finished. He came and he let his dropping go right on my head, 'Oh, no, it can't be!' But it was. I could have killed the blooming thing.

There's a really little small bird. We sometimes called the bigger ones *ningaris** and they go around in flocks, hundreds of them. They're finches. But this little bird is much smaller. It's a wren. The body's only the size of an ordinary egg, and they'd just make this terrible noise until they got you away from maybe sacred sites, maybe danger. Whatever it was, they'd more or less push you back to safety, back down the creek of course, but it was common. When I ran away from my husband that's what'd happened. Sometimes I'd go to sleep in the creek, just tired of running, but always some bird would be around.

I think there's a real connection between birds and Aboriginals, because different birds can tell you different things. Well the magpie, he comes in flocks at a time when some people have bad luck. In really big flocks and they sit all over. There's a butcherbird, which is a bigger bird than the magpie but very much the same. He's a warning. He used to warn my aunties of danger and travelling Aboriginals too you know. What we called *djinigubbies* or bad people was the thing that caused that. The butcherbirds would cry at night. I don't know whether it's what Noongar people call the 'death bird'. See, different culture. It could be.

If we hear a crow at night that's a sign of bad luck. Crows never call at night. But this butcherbird, once he starts shouting and shouting all night it creates a fear amongst the old people. Well in our family anyway. My aunty would never let me sleep. I had to stay awake because she reckons the *djinigubbies* would never come near her if a child was awake. She had me awake many nights. They wouldn't go near us because they didn't touch children. But I don't know. I've known people over in Kalgoorlie way that didn't care whether the people were kids or not. Ours is quite different I think. That was her ideas of the butcherbird giving us that warning. That noise went on and on and sometimes now that I'm older I think Aboriginal people could copy that bird. There's some strange noises we get even here, a different bird I've never heard before in my life.

But the birds have a connection without a doubt. They not only can warn Aboriginal people but they can also warn white people. I mean you look at a flock of birds fly up all of a sudden, well naturally you think there's something that's making them afraid. But usually the one that is most friendly is probably the willie wagtail because he's very much a loner. He's alone and he comes and visits you, and just depends on which way you think about the willie wagtail whether he's bad news or good news. But I tend to talk to them and they show by their actions if they want that conversation, because they fly in and out and everywhere about. That's really funny when they come.

The willie wagtail is always known as a messenger. Warning messenger, but that messenger isn't always a bearer of bad news. It could be but I think from our way, you just talk to them and they're your friend. There's nothing I've seen that's really bad.

They taught us how to track the emus. In the bush on rainy days that's usually the time the emus are nesting and they've got eggs. So on rainy days we looked for the tracks. They can track the emus a long distance or a short distance, but they usually lay within a five kilometre range of the same place each year. It wouldn't even be five kilometres. When they're close to their nest they run round and round, and circle the nest in case of foxes or some sort of predators. You often see that, where they're running and chasing something. When they want to go into their nest, because there's quite a wide circle around it, they tiptoe on the nails of their feet and you can see a little prick in the sand. They tiptoe and go into the nest, so you can't track them unless you know about that tiptoe.

The emu is very close with Aboriginals in lots of ways. You can coax them. If they see you put a little baby down that's just crawling or something on the ground and let him kick, that emu will come right in to see what's going on in a mother-like way. Of course it runs away if you frighten it, but it's a sticky-beak in that way, coming to see what's wrong with that baby.

Telepathy

Did I tell you what I thought about mental telepathy? Aboriginals could use that, and the white man of course gave it the name mental telepathy as we know it now. They used mental telepathy and astral travel. You could transport yourself in spirit to certain places and you could see those people. I think it's quite easily done. With the concentration of the mind you can master that into talking with the people and they would somehow contact you. I really don't know how well they could do that, because there were no telephones, there was nothing, but they knew everything. When my grandmother wanted her eldest daughter (Aunty Eva), she used sign language, but they knew what it was. Somehow Aunty Eva knew there was something wrong. She didn't know that her mother was dying. They wrote or scratched that date and time up on the trees or the tent they were in, and it was that good their knowledge of things.

My uncle had a brother in the First World War over in the Middle East and he got shell-shocked. This is Arthur Harris. He was shell-shocked and they knew that he was injured. I don't know how it happened truly. There was no phone. There was no way for them to know. But the two sisters back in Paynes Find knew there was something wrong. Aunty Eva, she said her brother-in-law Arty was fighting in the Middle East, and he got shell-shocked and he came in the tent and said, 'Eva. Eva.' So with that she wrote the exact time and the date, on the wall of the tent. He was in hospital of course and they were bringing him home. When they finally did find out that he was wounded in action they found out it was exactly that time that she wrote down. There are things like that they've mastered. I have to say Aboriginals have got that instinct. I can tell myself.

If you're suddenly worried — I do this quite often with my family and I wonder what they're doing, the next thing I'll get a phone call, bet your bottom dollar. It never misses. On another occasion a few years ago, my stepson died in Geraldton. I had a wagon, but somebody took a loan of it and they broke the ignition. So we were trying to fix it up for the funeral. Anyway it took too long. But people saw me at that funeral and they argued with me blind. I said, 'I couldn't go because the car was broken down.' 'No Aunty, you ask, they saw you there.' I said, 'They never saw me. I couldn't get there.' I think they still believe it. It was probably me in spirit, I don't know, I wanted to go there badly.

Some of the things that you compare with modern day happenings, words and things, it's something that Aboriginal people have dealt with all their lives since the beginning of time, and it's not new. Nothing is new, only that the whitefellers put a name to these things. People can sing you, mentally. They can sit down five or six hundred kilometres away and their spirits will come to you and you'll acknowledge that. In your sleep maybe you'll meet that person and talk. That's some things that happened.

My young grandson not long ago, last year [2006], he said, 'Oh Nanna I come to see you about something.' 'What was that?' He said, 'I must have been dreaming but this big black man came to me. He walked straight in and he said hullo to me and then he touched me on the shoulder. He said to me, "You right, you Widi." Nanna there was something wrong with his hand and he was a big feller, tall, big muscly feller. But he had something wrong with his hand.' And I couldn't help it, I had to laugh cos my uncle had that hand. He'd been dead over twenty or thirty years. He used to fight the police and all that. When he came and touched my grandson on the shoulder and just said, 'You right, you Widi,' he wasn't scared.

Sometimes I get some sort of messages from somewhere and when I wake up in the morning I know the answers. I'm sure my old Uncle Tom Phillips, he's got a lot to do with it. He used to tell us a lot of stories when we were kids.

The kid thought he was dreaming. But when he said, 'I have to ask because this man had a sore hand, something was wrong with it,' well

I knew straight away who it was. He was one of the law men from up there, Tom, my mother's brother, younger uncle. He went through the law. Only one uncle really missed out, that was the one that was married. Tom's fingers were twisted back, he was born like that. Things like that you know, disabilities, when you're born with them you're special people mostly, and can defend and have all those things when you pass into law. Unbelievable but it happened.

The fair-haired girl

Did I ever tell you about the fair-haired girl up on the Murchison out from Cue? Well somewhere there close to it is Walga Rock. It's a comparison I always make — white people have a God that's everywhere, and they believe God will come back and save them. Well in a way that's the same belief of an Aboriginal. The likeness is so much. Up north they've got the Wandjina. At Cue they've got this fair-haired girl, a half-caste girl that was born in the tribe. Whether her mother just mated with a whitefeller or not I don't know. But she painted a ship on the wall of the cave that's still there, though I think other people go along and touch it up. Because that was always the idea when they painted anyway, that people would touch it up every so often and do their rounds and look after those sacred sites and things, it wasn't unusual.

I saw her in my visions a few times. She was always dancing. I tried to catch her but I couldn't. She'd disappear. It was so strange. I was telling one of the old fellers about it and he said, 'Oh girl, you shouldn't be seeing that.' I said, 'Why?' 'No no no, shouldn't do that. Ah never,' I was young you know. I said, 'Well why not? Everybody's the same.' 'No,' he said, 'only special people see her.' My sister-in-law is that girl reincarnated. I didn't know that she went through the law. People know it. All the Wongis know it. When she was young she came to Mount Magnet at sixteen and immediately I knew her face, and never seen her before in my life. I dreamed about her before she came there.

I must tell you this because you can document it. I don't really want to tell too much on it but. My sister-in-law (Valerie, my brother Kevin Lewis' wife) was put through the law in Kalgoorlie about ten years ago. They took her and gave her some things and they told her, 'You're not a Wongi, and you're not a Noongar. You go back up there to them Widi people, that's where you come from.' And they sent her to that Wilgi Mia, Walga Rock they call it. There's a picture of that half-caste girl on that wall, she had to go back and shift that little girl out of that cave, the Kangaroo cave they call it. It's near Mount Magnet. This is really dangerous talk I suppose. Anyway she had to go in, because when they took her first and put her through the law they made her sit outside this big red cave. And the woman that took her, and another little blonde-headed girl, went in the cave while she sat and watched. So when she'd been up here and that — she took some ochre, I've got some of that there — they told her she had to go back up there and get that little girl out. They said she was safe [because] she's a special person.

They whisked her away through this astral travel and she came to this cave. She told me, 'It was like I just went *zoom*,' and she said she was at the cave so she had to walk in. But she said, 'You know Joan, that big Kangaroo? He just stepped aside to let me in. And when I went in, that little girl was in there and I said, "Come on, you got to come out of here, you're not allowed here." "Oh," she said, "I don't want to leave."' I'd love for her to tell you, I really would. 'And,' she said, 'this little girl wouldn't go, and Joan she's a pretty little girl. She did look like me but she was prettier than me. She had two big dimples in her cheeks.' So she said, 'Come on, come with me now,' and that little girl ran and she jumped on her back, and my sister-in-law carried that *moban* on her back. But she said she has to get off. She can follow her but she can't carry her. That's her *moban*. And that's her area and people.

Well it's sitting on her back, in this Dreamtime. But it's so strange. You wouldn't understand it I guess but it's perfectly real. It's like that story I gave you about the mushroom stone. It comes to me and it's so real, and I wonder, 'What the hell am I doing?' You know, 'How can I come to these stories?' It'll be there always to protect her, this little girl, but she said, 'I can't carry her around all the time!' It's very comical. She said, 'Joan, you wouldn't believe it.' And she can't bring herself too either cos she's been educated — I mean she's been reared up down here and that — and she said, 'Oh, other people they wouldn't understand,' her family and that, 'they wouldn't understand what I'm saying but I know you do.' She gets a real laugh out of it.

She was telling me about it and I said, 'In that cave?' 'Oh,' she said, 'it's just red.' I said, 'That's Walga Rock they call it, where the ochre is.' Wilgi Mia rather, not Walga Rock. Walga Rock's got the painting on it. But Wilgi Mia, that's the story I was telling you about the big red Kangaroo that chased all the smaller ones away and took over all the food, and when they killed him he rolled down the hill and he fell into that hole, and the blood is the red ochre. It's associated with that girl.

She was married to my dead brother. They had a family, four girls and one boy. The family name is Lewis. That's my maiden name. The other girl, they told her, was Valerie's sister that went in the cave. Whether she was a human girl or a spirit, one never knows. Could be a spirit, could be anything. I'm not sure and I wouldn't like to talk about it really.

Reading the country

I know a lot that I shouldn't know and people think I'm making it up, but it comes out, a lot of things. I mean, when I go on a site clearance up the bush and the kids go out looking for the artefacts and anything to do with Aboriginal inheritance and sacred sites, I can tell them where to go. I don't know how but I can tell them and they'll find it. Never been before. But you got to learn to read the country.

When my young grandson Wesley was only twelve we were going past a rock and he said, 'Nanna, did you see that?' I said, 'What?' (Cos he's training himself to look out.) He said, 'Those rocks are just like a big turtle sitting on the top.' It had legs and a shell and a head, and it truly was like a big turtle. I said, 'Well if I was holding Native Title to this country it sure would be a sacred site.' You don't have to have someone tell you, because what's there is part of the Dreamtime. It's a symbol that was put there long before people. It's the shape of a turtle sitting on a rock sunning himself, so real you could take a photo of it and say 'see the big turtle there'. Like most animals turtles have the natural instinct to return to the same place every year to nest, the same pattern year after year. I once painted a small picture that shows the turtle travelling to and from the nesting ground.

The other day two boys went up with archaeologists and they spotted a huge amount of artefacts. They kept looking around and they ended up following the trail. It went to surface water, fresh water, and then it went in to a cave. So the old people must have been living in that area. They had their water there, their artefacts, they had everything. At the front entrance to that cave was a big rock. The caves are usually made out of granites and sometimes hard dirt, but that rock is foreign to there. They transported that rock to that place. You don't know where it comes from, and you don't get to know either, because it's a rock that they use in law — circumcision, cutting things up, their food, their animals, everything, and there's all these little chips around. It's not hard to read what it's doing there.

I mean you go into the bush and you're sitting on an iron ore hill, you don't expect to find other kinds of stone. They are different colours, and you just know they don't belong there. It's like the trees I told you about, they didn't belong there. But there were five of them I counted last time I went up. Going well, got all their little nuts, and it's all through the country, up the bush there out in the hills. They're also seen in Wiluna and north of Wiluna. Those are the trees that they use as drugs to catch food. They carry them on and still use it today. They didn't always use spears and all that jazz you know, what they put in the historical evidence.

Lots of Aboriginal people are born with instinct. We could tell by the wind many, many things. We could tell if there was going to be a loss, a death, and we could whistle the wind to bring the water up, and fresh air. There were ground paintings that were painted for food. Wait for the sunrise, and before dawn that wind will come along. When it comes along, whichever way that wind blew it would take the painting with it and then they'd follow it and get the food they've painted. That's why everyone in that tribe, they'd be somewhere close to a station and people wonder, 'Oh I wonder where them fellers went?' They'd go with the wind before the rising sun. In the morning before the sun rises there's always a wind. They'd get up before that sunrise and they'd follow that wind and they'd find what they painted. That's how they did it, a mental force. There was a lot of belief in the wind I can tell you. The wind had so much power. So many things they could tell you.

There's also an instincts of things, like a sense. If you were in a sacred site you'd know it. Just by instinct you'd know you had to get out of that area. Sometimes birds would chase you out. There were all sorts of things you could connect with that showed you something. If you were looking at some rocks and, just the whole area you know, the darkness in some places was really dangerous, and then there were open spaces and you'd always have a weird, weird warning. But once that warning went from you, from the wind and everything else that's surrounding you, you'd be right. You'd more or less know that you're free and nothing will happen.

We had lots of fear as well, a sixth sense of sacred sites and places you couldn't go. But sometimes we were not told about it until after we actually went there. Groups of trees and that, when you walk in, it can be a hot day, no wind, no nothing. The minute you go into those trees they start blowing wind and you'd get a weird feeling. Little willy-willy as we call them. They come up everywhere and come straight to us, all sorts of signs like this we were taught. Whistling the wind up, that was the main one. That was the best one. On hot days when we used to go out the bush to have dinner the kids used to get in the tanks, so you couldn't drink that water. But we'd whistle the wind for water to be pumped up and just like that the wind would come, and the fresh cold water came up from underneath the earth. It's just unbelievable.

We were up the bush there and two times we went back to this place where they built a mining camp, and no one could sleep. I was only disturbed twice. The first night the air conditioner went silly, it was like a truck roaring. 'Gee that's funny,' but I couldn't reach it so I said, 'Oh blow it, I'll go back to sleep.' But in the morning everyone woke up and my cousin reckoned it was coming up out of the ground as well, bumping underneath the camps where they had their mine. Bumping there, bumping all around, knock knock here, knock knock. All I got was this loud noise like a truck coming through the air conditioner. So that was all right. We went back again after and I got really, really sick. I didn't know what was wrong and I thought I might have had a bit of a heart attack. But then when we left that area I was fine.

This was at Mindja mining camp. When we were going up that way again I said, 'No we can't go there and stay.' My cousin asked me, 'Why?' I told her, 'No. We can't go there. That place is built on a sacred site.' I still believe it was too, only we never ever saw it before. It was an uncanny experience. We all knew it and nobody said anything to anybody on the night. But in the morning it all came out. Everybody never had a sleep, oh wicked! We don't go back there. I knew for next time I wasn't allowed there.

They're opening it up again because the gold price has gone up. It's not far from Golden Grove out from Yalgoo. I don't care if you write that name in cos it doesn't touch certain people.

We also went up the bush and tried to do a bit of looking around ourselves and it was nothing but a disaster. We had a 4WD Prada. Well that thing caused us more than enough trouble. It was using petrol like it was going out of style. We had no peace till we came back, it was the trailer we hired to go up on the hills, the blooming thing started making this horrible noise. I didn't know what it was. Then we found out the axle or something was broken — a hundred and forty dollars to go from Yalgoo to Wubin. When we were out there we went camping. The boys went to see if they could get a roo just before sundown, and me and all the kids and the girls were there. They had a couple of cars and a caravan. I was sitting on this big rock with my back to the creek and the hill. I looked up in the sky and there came this, like a fire. But when it got over us it opened up. It was coming over the hill. When it got over the top of us it spread round and just disappeared. But the next morning the trailer stuffed up. Anyway we got it going, then we got so far and we were all talking about it. Someone said, 'Oh, what you reckon?' I said, 'You're not meant to come. We're going back before we get there, back to Yalgoo. We never had so much trouble in our lives.'

It just sort of takes over, the spiritual side of things, and it makes you afraid, and once you get afraid you've got to move. If you don't move, you know somebody might appear or a spiritual warning comes. Once they warn you spiritually, well you've got to move. You can't stay unless you are a person that's been through the law and you're meant to stay.

Lots of little things happen, like a handful of tiny gravel stones, they were pelted into my room in Paynes Find. It was a rotten stinking hot night and we had to have the door open. I heard them being thrown and I said to the boys when they came back from the shop, 'Can you see any stones here? Turn the light on and just look,' because I can't see too well in the night. One of the boys said, 'Oh, I'll camp in that bed over there.' So they did. I couldn't find those stones in the morning. I went back home two days later and I opened my bag and there were the stones. How they got in my handbag I don't know but they were the same little gravel stones. I think it's a warning that people are there. Then the other night when I went to sleep in the car I just got up in the morning and they were there. Stones. Those little pebbles, gravel. I don't know how it got on my shoes when I was asleep but they were all there and they were also in my bag. [They were shown during recording.] It's not a danger sign. It's telling you that the spirits are there. The old people used to say, 'Oh, very danger, don't go there. Very danger.' Their English you know was a bit rough. Everyone knew what they were saying. My old Uncle Tom was the biggest leader of the lot.

I love the bush. The bush is my home. But I have also a fear for the spiritual side of things. It's not plain sailing I mean, when you're taught all the instincts. Like I said before, if you have that thing that would tell you not to go there, not to go anywhere near it, well you didn't do it. There were so many different things that we used to do. It's probably why you go back on them and think about what happened. That's a long way back but I still remember the stories coming from the old people and the things they taught us that we weren't allowed to do at night and during the day — where to go, and the noises we had to listen for — to obey the law whatever the reason.

Wudatjis

Only twenty-three ks [kms] east of Morawa there's a huge range of hills called Wudatji Hills, or Koolanooka Hills. It's a big sacred site. That's where the spirits have lived all the time I've known it. I don't know that there was an Aboriginal name. We just called it Koolanooka Hills but it didn't really have a name. Or if it did, we weren't taught those things. See my mother was put through the Moore River Settlement, and when they talked, my mother and my aunty, they used to whisper. God knows who they feared, but it was as though they were afraid of somebody listening.

Those hills are the home of the *wudatjis**. We weren't allowed to stay out too late after dark because of the *wudatjis*. I remember we used to leave a great big log burning on the fire all night. Cos I was a stickybeak I asked, 'Why was this log burning?' During the winter my mother would always leave a big fire for them to warm themselves and you could hear them calling and coming in, but we weren't allowed to look. We all had to be quiet because the little fellers came in there to get warm. When they were coming and calling, it could have been a fox, it could have been anything, but the noise was there. I don't know whether the old people meant to frighten us so we'd go to bed or not, but we were scared.

In other countries they used to call them leprechauns but they must have been there. They found the latest things, hobbits just up north of us, and there's the New Guinea pygmies. So why not *wudatjis*? It is true I know, because my Mum said, 'Keep them warm when they come down from the hills.' They'd make a noise to let us know that they were there coming down, just shouting, what we call yakkaiing*. It was really strange.

They're ripping apart Koolanooka Hills. That's a bad case. There's a big damper-like hill, and you see a wedge come out of it. It's as though somebody's got a knife and cut it, and out pops this round circle in the stone. When you're here on top, not on Mount Gibson but the ranges you know, and you're looking down you see a whole different place hundreds of metres down. It's like it's below sea level it's just so far down. You see the level of the ground. This is in Koolanooka near

Morawa. Those hills are so lovely it's very hard to say yes to mining companies. It was just one of those places we weren't allowed to go to.

There's something in the 'nooka'*. It's Aboriginal for 'water' I think. Yandanooka, Koolanooka, Merkanooka — there were heaps of them that meant something to do with water. So a lot of names came out of that place from Dongara across to Morawa. There are some beautiful places we see that 'beautiful people' would turn their noses up at.

Women's law

I know where there's women's business in the Morawa–Yalgoo area and other big corroboree grounds, and hidden things in different places. My mother told me about them. There are a lot of shady places you can't go to. There's women's law as well. Like, the women aren't allowed there with the men, and the men aren't allowed where the women are. It's a strange world I suppose and people get the idea, 'Oh the law's dying out so you can do what you like.' But a lot of people get sick from it, that's how they're told where they're not allowed to go. The law's not really dying out. Never will. I don't believe it will. Old people get scared, but I have never been scared up there all around.

I've seen a birthing place, when I was on the edge of the granite — I don't know what other people think happened, that they had their babies in caves only. Maybe they did but I saw out in the open on the side of the granite where they'd used a tool. The main one I think where the babies were born was a big perfect circle. They'd done that into the granite. There were seven all together. But the one main one was about a metre across or a metre and a half — it was huge — for somebody to have a baby in. Then in the middle around it were these oval shaped holes. They were a bit weathered because they were only small, and the rain you know, coming down. I hope it's still there. I hope the cutting stone's still there. I wanted to take it, but I didn't. There are so many things that go through your mind. They were only about eighteen inches [45.7 cm] long but they were ovalish.

Then about twenty metres away there's a half circle of stones and a cutting stone between which marked where they took the afterbirth and buried it. The only way anybody could possibly prove us wrong would be to test where that sand is, see if that afterbirth's still there today. Of course we didn't bother to take the stone away but I sometimes regret it, because a lot of people go to the granites and have a good time and throw stones around and that, and I haven't been there for a good six years, maybe more. But I often regret it. I don't think we ever made it a sacred site.

My brother went to a place where there's a hill for women's business. The blokes with us said, 'No you can't go on to that, you can't go there. It's women's business and the men have to stay down.' But he ignored that and he went up there. Well he was so sick for months and months. We were told by somebody he wouldn't be able to walk. He suffered. He couldn't walk and he got very sick. We nearly lost him a couple of times. It turned out he had something like legionnaire's disease, in the lungs as well. They told us when you go up to the top of the hill a wind would come. Well it was a stinking hot day and we were more or less petering out, no water, no wind. But once we were at the top the wind came to let us know that these spirits are there. It's women's business and that spirit was quite angry we'd gone there. Definitely those men were not allowed there, but two of them went up and they ended up sick. The other one went off his head for a while. Hopefully he's a bit normal now. My brother Willie died. From that time on he went downhill.

That place is just absolutely riddled with drill holes, they're going to mine it, and I told them from the beginning that it was a sacred site. Well they ignored that and they went ahead and drilled. Then my cousins came along and said, 'Don't you touch the southern end.' We allowed them to have six drill holes and when we went back there it was just riddled with holes and there were roads everywhere. Then the last trip they went into the southern end and drilled and I had a row with them. But the government believed that we shouldn't be having any say. I had to go up that hill and say Aboriginal words to coax that old woman [spirit] down off the Kararra hill, to remind her. But there you are.

Law

I saw things I'm sure those people in Mount Magnet haven't seen. I knew a lot before that cos I was a sticky-beak. I used to go and find these things. I'd go back and tell my husband but he'd say, 'Oh well, you know that no Littles are to go through the law here.' I said, 'Why?' And he said, 'Because we don't come from here, and they're not allowed to put us through the law.'

If you did the wrong thing and you broke that law you'd suffer for it with your life. There was no putting you in jail. Well people ran but they could have ended up like the Sturt Pea couldn't they? Run and run and never come back. People chase them. They go into exile, pushed out of the land not to come back. That explains a lot too you know when people move on.

One young feller had to get out of there because he did something wrong. Ten years he came over here [Perth]. He was married to one of my son's people on his father's side. Ten years later he went back, long time to be banished. Those fellers there, they were terrible law people. Not terrible, but they had no fear of people you know. They're half-castes but they dare not disobey that law. And they couldn't marry. This here modern day thing now what's going on and people claim to follow law, were never allowed to invade. Never, that was a no-no. They picked out the skins when they went through the law and they told them you're allowed to have this one, this one and that one but not that one.

And the women's law I was talking about was really a rough thing. In our way the people who did those things [punished law breakers] were called *djinigubbies*. Because *djina* was the foot and the *gabi* was water, and walking in the water was to cover their tracks. They used to go out before it rained so the rain would come and cover their tracks. That's what we were told. They did their dirty work in the rain or wet weather. Nobody could track them through the mud because the water would wash it away. In other places they call them featherfoot because they'd make a shoe out of the fine feathers of an emu. How they ever did it I don't know, unless they tied it together with some sort of sinew. I've seen those shoes they make. They have them in the blooming museum. It's so ridiculous for people to stand up and say, 'Oh that's all finished now. They don't do that any more.' But they do. It carries on. It doesn't stop.

To the blackfeller uranium was used for killing purposes. They put that in the drink and kill them, sends them off. Everything in their stomach and body collapses. I had a nephew down here that came down from Carnarvon. Him and his mate went and had an early morning 'livener' they called it, and they both had a drink out of the one bottle. Bloke gave them a drink. They ended up in hospital that afternoon with the same symptoms, the same things wrong with them. They flew them down here a couple of days after. Their bodies were in perfect condition when they went in to hospital, but later on everything started to shut down. His mother called me in there then because he was really dying. They got some other people to send their things down. They saved the one that was dying at the time and all his fingers and his toes were dead, cut off. He's still alive. But my nephew — we used to call him Cockroach — they couldn't save him. They saved one but not the other.

It poisoned everything in the body. The doctor called me and the mother outside and said, 'They think there is something strange about it. We don't know what's caused it.' He didn't know how to say it and he said, 'Do you think this must be some Aboriginal thing?' It was exactly that. So he said, 'Now we know what we're fighting.' But it was too late. It was a poison that was put in the bottle they drank from, but there's an antidote for it. They use uranium I'm telling you. I mean that's often been the case, and it depends on what you put in the alcohol. If you're a drinker you got to be careful of people, of blackfellers chasing you.

Another thing they use is a pink in colour. I don't know why, but that stuff changed pink in beer. That'd be a good test eh? *Giddi-giddi* is a powder they sing people with, they rub the powder over things. Say this woman really likes oranges and some man wants that woman, he'll rub it on there and give an orange to that one to sing her.

Singing the law back

I saw a corroboree when it started off in the summer time. For the dance that night they'd trample on that ground all day. I saw it in Roebourne at one time and I said, 'What are they doing that for?' It was because they had to have the dust to fly over their bodies when they danced. It was really pretty. They got all these new leaves off the gum trees, all the tender young things, and they'd put them on their arms, on their legs, head, everywhere for decoration. They'd rub this red ochre in with some sort of oil, I guess emu oil, and their bodies were shining with this red ochre. They'd put a little bit of white ochre on, whatever their symbols were, and dance. It was a sight like you've never seen before.

The whole process, they had a group of men and women sitting — this is when they brought these boys back from the initiation — in a horseshoe shape they went through. This old woman was a leader of the whole dance. They danced. It took them about an hour and a half to come five hundred metres. They'd take a few steps and they'd stop and she'd shout and they'd dance, and she'd dance around the boys. They'd go on and on and on. This happened repeatedly when she finally got them to where all these people were sitting head down. Each of those boys had to walk, and they'd rub their sides, their ears or somewhere there with their hands and chanting all the time. The women would take a turn in the dancing too, and they'd go and lay the men back and rub their breasts on them, blow in their ears and oh God whatever. It went on for hours. It started around four o'clock in the morning — up the north it was just daylight, you know light — and it wouldn't end for hours. You'd just be sitting like in a trance watching everything. It's something I would never have missed out on, and I'd like to see it again. That was in Roebourne but it's not much difference.

I was a woman then, about thirty-seven, thirty-eight. My daughter's forty. She was a little two year old so it'd be thirty-eight years ago, and her birthday is today [Wednesday, 19 September 2007]. Nicky was about three or four years old and she was born in '67. [So the corroboree took place around 1970–71.]

It started when these blokes that I knew — I always was a traveller — got me to pick them up in Geraldton. They came around and they said, 'Oh, this person's lived there. You might know him from Mount Magnet.' Oh gee they were in a pickle. He said, 'We've got a car and we got some money.' He had a few thousand dollars, but he got into an accident. He said, 'I know you got a licence. Look can you just come and get the car out of the police station? We have to have someone with a licence.' Well the police station was only two hundred metres down the road from where I was staying in Geraldton. So I went and got the car and then I could see they wanted to say something else. They said, 'Oh, could you come on a holiday with us?' 'Me?' I said, 'No, I've got kids. I can't do that.' So he said, 'Come on, we'll look after the kids.' I knew him very well. He promised me, 'I'll look after the kids and they won't starve. They won't go without anything and I'll give them a holiday.'

Well look it was comical in one way because there's not one of the blokes had a blooming driver's licence and they had all been drunk the night before. So I said, 'Oh all right.' 'Oh, when can we go?' 'Oh,' I said, 'in the morning I'll take you.' So I got the car and they just all camped out the back. There were about four of them. I got the kids ready, just chucked the bag in and a couple of rugs. But being summer time it was stinking hot, we probably didn't need them. All right, the kids went to sleep in the boot of the car, and nobody else was to get in there. They made the rules and that was fine, and the kids had their cool drink and nobody was to drink it. It was really funny you know. The kids' water, the kids must come first cos I suppose they were all fathers.

So away we went. And they were drunk the night before, but we pulled up the other side of Geraldton on the way to Carnarvon and one feller, oh he was blooming still hung over. He said, 'I have to get some water too. I don't want to drink the kids' water. Pull up at the first [wind]mill and have a feed.' There was one quite close to the road so I pulled in. He had a cool drink of water poor feller, and I was watching him blowing, and he got drunk immediately. He was blowing you know, from the water, like a lizard out of a waterhole. Anyway the water made him drunk. It revived all the alcohol. I said, 'Well I'll go back from here because these fellers don't want to behave.' But I really couldn't, and the other thing was I wanted to meet my cousin up in Roebourne. I knew he was living there. We went through Port Hedland too. I ended up going cos I had control of everything. They gave me control, the owner of the money and the vehicle. He was a good old feller. He was the one got drunk mind you. He was, 'Oh sorry, I'm sorry, I'm sorry.'

Away we went on and pulled in to Carnarvon, and I went around to my old uncle's place. They were all right, a bit scared cos they'd never been north before. But the people were all right to them. They were good to them. They were really scared. They were like little boys. Oh I had a good laugh cos I knew them all.

When we got going on to Port Hedland, away we went straight up the highway. It was really funny cos I'd never been any further than Carnarvon myself. We called in to Onslow and it was strange. The Aboriginal reserve was right on the water's edge. There was no sand. It's all pebbles on the beach. It was different. Got a bit of sand, you know as you're going in, but the beach itself is all pebbly and shells and whatever. Anyway we went in to Onslow to see how it was structured and someone said, 'I'll get a couple of drinks eh?' 'Oh do what you like,' cos I was driving. I wasn't drinking or anything, and the kids got cool drinks, got a feed.

Away we went again and we got to Karratha. Well that was like a real bloody police town. It was when it first started you know. The whole thing was owned by Hamersley Iron. Oh God what a disaster! I had no idea there was such a thing. They had all the infrastructure I suppose you call it, and lights everywhere. Anyway we got lost in the whole mining sector. Everything was weird and they were all panicking you know. They were like they were in a maze, went to the panic button and pressed that. One was saying, 'Just listen to Joan. She knows.' I didn't know anything but I said, 'Oh we'll just read the street signs.' So it took us right back to the main road and on the main road was this blooming pub. 'Oh we'll have to get a drink here sis. Camp the night over on the beach?' I said, 'Oh whatever.' You know they got a carton each. They bought me a carton too. Well I used to drink too those days and it was stinking hot anyway.

I used to drink. I was never squeaky clean don't worry about that. Everybody has done something wrong. But I was never meant to drink because it didn't take me long to wake up. I woke up with a sick head that was a start. About six years I drank. Then I saw my kids growing up and I thought, 'Ah, they're men and women now so I can't do that. I have to respect my kids.'

So I'm sitting on this carton when all of a sudden this Land Rover pulled up and I saw these blokes get down. They had brown khaki clothes on that looked real nice. I had no idea — you see not being from up there — that the uniforms had changed and the police were in khakis. They got out, 'How you going there mate?' 'Real good.' 'Ah yeah, where you heading?' 'Oh just having a rest before tomorrow. We'll go along to Roebourne.' 'Oh right.' Anyway they walked around in a circle. Blokes were talking and everyone was tired. Nobody had had a drink, so they couldn't charge them then for drink. We only just got there.

He said, 'Right you can all come with me.' Oh I was getting mad cos we'd also picked up this other girl that was going up that way, and a blind man was amongst the fellers that originally came. He only could feel your arm to know who you were. He was brainy. He played the guitar and everything. He's still alive I might add. I haven't seen him since.

'Oh well you're allowed to stay,' the policeman said to me and the kids, and the girl and the blind feller. 'The rest have got to go to jail.' I said, 'Whatever for?' and he said, 'Disorderly conduct.' I said, 'You can't do that. They didn't do anything wrong.' 'Oh yes we can,' he said. I said, 'Well when are they coming out? Cos I haven't got any money. I'm only their driver.' I started panicking. I had no idea that people could be like that, you know, the police, and in a country town like that, not a clue.

Anyway they came up to where we were in the morning and said, 'You've got to move along.' I said, 'Oh I can't do that. That'd be stealing you know, this bloke's car.' 'Oh,' he said, 'he knows.' I said, 'How do you make that out?' 'Well,' he said, 'I told him that you were going.' I said, 'But I can't go cos I haven't got the money to go on with petrol,' and I said, 'I can't just take somebody else's car.' 'Yes you can,' he said. 'You pull up over to that petrol station,' he said, 'and I'll get you the petrol to go on to Roebourne.' 'I don't know where Roebourne is.' He said, 'I'll show you.' We went over there, I pulled up and I said, 'What about this petrol?' Well those days he got me four dollars worth of petrol. That was nearly a full tank up there, and being so cheap it was about ten cents or thirteen cents. Roebourne was only twenty-two ks [kms]. I was fuming and I said, 'Oh God I'm taking this man's car, and all his grog was chucked in too.' Oh no, then the cops took most of it.

As soon as I got to Roebourne I went round to Welfare and things, and I met my cousin so I was alright. They spent seven days in jail for nothing. They did nothing. And the cops took their grog and all. Disorderly conduct that was their charge. I got the Welfare and that in Roebourne to ring up because I said, 'I just can't take off with somebody's car.' 'They got seven days. You won't see them for seven days.' I said, 'I've got the car, what am I going to do?' They said, 'Oh well, do you know anyone here?' I said, 'I've got a cousin here, and I'll find him.' But he was on the reserve.

Those people at that time in Roebourne, it didn't matter if they didn't have a tent or a camp or anything, they just lived as they would have in the bush. You'd go over this big creek — beautiful river past there — on to this reserve, just a big open flat with a couple of trees on it. Everybody just camped everywhere. They had a toilet block and a couple of camps but apart from that they just rolled their swags out everywhere. The big corroboree I told you about earlier started in the next couple of days. Those blokes did actually get back just in time.

So we were all sitting in the car and someone said, 'Oh where are we going to camp?' I said, 'Let's get out of it! It's a bloody law camp!' 'Oh no, we can't go yet. We got to wait till the bank opens for money.' So we went up the Port Hedland road and I said, 'Look, I'm getting tired and I have to have a sleep.' 'Well, hang on a minute,' they reckoned, 'We'll make a camp here and you and the kids can sleep in the car,' cos it was a station wagon, and the other girl was with us.

But before we went anywhere we were surrounded by Aboriginal people spears and all. They knocked on the window and I thought, 'Oh God. What's the matter?' 'You got to shift from here girl.' I didn't know what to say. I said, 'Why? What for?' 'No. No good, you got to go. We're law. We're law,' they said. I looked at the others and said, 'Start the car up and let's go!' They didn't know the place and neither did I. So anyway, I took off and I went a little bit further, and blow me down they followed us. They said, 'If you don't go we're goin' to smash the car up and everything.' I headed straight back to town to the reserve, and blow me down if the bloody thing wasn't right there at my cousin's camp. That's where it was all powdered up ready. I was on the Dream, like the track, on the track where they had to bring them back see. That's why.

I was watching them from far away but you could hear them singing, and this old woman going round and round. All of a sudden they'd stop singing and she'd shout, 'Ahhhhh,' round. It was amazing I tell you. I don't know how many times she did that but it seemed like forever. And the way that they did — they somehow must have known how many steps or something to take, how many yards to them, and they had to stop and do that dance. But those poor fellers then [those being initiated], they'd taken all this food. The other people built a bough shed that fast for them, and cos there's no trees close there they had to go out and get them [branches]. The shelter for them had everything there. They brought bags of flour and sugar and tea for them. Meat was getting brought by the truckload you may as well say. That was to feed these special people. There were four of them I think, four or five at a time. They had skirts put on them, and they're walking along holding the skirts away, head down, young fellers. It was that real!

It was a sight I'd love to see again. After that they all broke up and they put the boys in this bough shed they made fresh. All the people were taking food like kangaroo meat, emu meat, flour, milk and sugar. Not milk. They didn't drink milk. Sugar and tea, everything. They had women making dampers for them. They were treated like kings. This is the respect I guess now I think about it, the respect for the law, how they did it.

The car went downtown to Roebourne — we were staying out near the reserve — and picked up another load of boys. This is around Christmas time they were taking them in and out. And if you were up to no good, they were telling me there, you'd get punished in a hard way, like they made initiation painful. But if you were docile and went and did what they told you, everything would be all right. Very strong, and I think that Roebourne law is still the same.

They'd kick it off up in Onslow and they'd walk. They'd bring another lot from Port Hedland. The oldest might be in the car driving along, but the blokes that had to go through the law, they walked. They had to walk every inch of the way. Roebourne was the centre point between Onslow and Port Hedland. But to go back now, you might see it. I don't know whether you'll ever see it again. It was proper law those days.

I'd love to go back to the places I've been. I've been all around Melbourne, Adelaide, all around up the north in Meekatharra and that. I've mixed with those old people and I've spoken to them. Lots of people knew me that I'd never seen before. You'd hear them shout, you know, and I understood what they said. But it was a long time ago, thirty years since I've been there. I used to understand what they were saying. I could hear them saying, 'These are my people.' 'Ah, I can see my people coming.' They'd sometimes be crying and sometimes they'd dance around and that.

I know that Aboriginals now are singing the law back, and that has to begin from right across, from the centre and come back through the tribes, because that's where the Beginning was, Ernabella. Very strong tribal people at Ernabella. I knew some people from there, law men. Some parts of the law are good. Other parts make your hair stand up. You know, it's just hard to believe that people did the things they did.

8.

Yarrna

I always wanted to paint when I was a kid. I used to try my hands at landscapes in acrylic. I suppose I could have gone on and done a little bit more, but marriage always gets in the way eh. I didn't ever do much. Always wanted to, and then came Native Title and I knew I could do it. It was not a matter of copying anyone. It was just a matter of — I saw Mick [Little] painting a bit and I thought, 'I can do that,' you know. He said, 'Well do it,' and he chucked a canvas at me. I said, 'Oh no worries.' He was shocked himself when I said I can do that. I knew I could do it. That was in the late 1970s.

I don't draw. I paint. I don't draw anything. I just paint it with the paint, and whatever figure comes out I modify it and do what I want. I put the paint on the brush and I start with maybe just a single line, and that's how it comes out. I don't draw or trace or use pencils. Only thing I've used a pencil on is the circle, and you might see it on a few where I've missed spots. I just draw it. I'm used to the animals, used to the figures. I know what they look like. Then, you know, I might put five toes on a *bungarra* and it probably only has three. But I always put five. The painting can take you as long as you want it to. If you want to do it quickly then do it quickly. I wouldn't mind a dollar for every dot though, cos there's a few dollars in there.

I love painting and the thing that's stopping me now is I haven't got a home. I've got the canvas and I've got the paints. The kids got stuck into them you know. The brushes there, I just keep my brushes for years. But I haven't any money to buy the paints and things. These ones here, unless you happen to get them at the salvage yard or something, they're very expensive cos that's pig bristles. They're the best brushes in the market. You can do anything with them, cut lines and all. I got to put my hand out and make my circle myself. Hold it like a pencil but curve it. I love painting. I could paint my life away, but I'd run out of stories and things. I always wanted to paint. I started in '79 I think.

I have a lot of paintings. Mine got one style and that. I don't use bright reds or pinks or purples or greens, because they don't belong to my country. You couldn't, you know. Like up north they can make a dye out of some green thing and they got green and purple, and that's what they use to do their basket weaving and different other things like that. Well we didn't have that, just used ochre colours. There's some lovely ochre from up the bush, the prettiest purple, dark rich purple you've ever seen. You can get green ochre, but it's rare and also it's sacred to Aboriginal people.

I don't have my own house. I've got canvases ready to be painted but no concentration and nowhere to sit down and paint. You got to have inspiration and I have that so many times in my mind, but I can't do anything about it. I've laid down at night and got up in the middle of the night and done something, and I won't stop until I've finished that painting. I got some big ones out in a friend's house in Ballajura, five foot by three foot. They were big, old now, twenty years old, a bit over twenty.

You know when that [Burswood] casino started, I could knock up a painting no worries and go to the casino. It was like free money. I used to sell it for three or four hundred dollars. I wish I had that money now instead of pushing it through the casino. Oh well, easy come easy go, and I was happy. I've got paintings at Helsinki where the big museum is. Emu eggs too, I carved plenty of them in my time. Before the America's Cup they were into carvings and paintings, boab nuts.

I painted under two different names. Aboriginal people call me Kalyudi. It's something to do with being black, the same as they used to call my son Kagul [Greg]. He was dark. *Kagul**, crow. A crow. That name sticks to him even today. That's the crow, a woman, Kalyudi, and I shortened it and called it Kalla, cos *kalla** means fire in our lingo. Those paintings there're in Japan. There were eight of them I sent over. They sold the lot, no worries. Waste I guess, but I was younger and I was on top of the world. But I didn't know what was to come.

Yarrna*, I stuck to that name. I just made it up because you're telling a good yarn. Aboriginal people they twist their 'r' so I said 'Yarrna.' That's the only reason I had when I just swung off it, off one name and went to the other. Then when they burnt me out over in Paris Way a whole lot of the paintings were destroyed. I had a couple left, and they got destroyed as well. But there you are, when I'm dead and gone they'll know that those kinds of colour paintings are my style.

A lot went to America. People took them, bought them. But then I didn't know their value. I just loved to paint. Then came the America's Cup. Well, my friend [Mick] he did this whole exhibition. I was thrilled with that. He had a thing at the Adelaide Festival exhibition as well, and I had my own thing by then too. Oh, Christ Almighty he didn't sell anything so we kept them, and I believe now myself he wasn't meant to sell them. They were done on boards, very first painting, and varnished. They were really good paintings. It's like putting boomerangs in an exhibition, to show your culture you know? It's a spiritual thing.

Four spirits

I went home from here [Hamilton Hill near Fremantle] up to my other son's house in the mid-afternoon and I just sat down and I did that painting. And when he came home he asked me, 'Why did you do that?' And I said, 'Well there were these fellers, I'm sick of them. They torment me every night so now I've caught them on canvas and they can't do that no more.' I laughed. But the spirit of colours goes with the — I mean any art critic will say you must have been terribly down when you did that painting, because it always shows, and it's scary isn't it? There's just something like a cobweb [in the lower right hand corner] keeping everything together. To me that's what it means. And the circle is the spirits from my country. They travel and they travel, and they keep travelling. But they're there all the time.

Then when I did that other little one today, they're of people from the past. People that I walked with probably and talked with. But they're people from the past and that. That's the lines I had to make. What a way to go! I get scared of myself sometimes. How could I come up with these things? I told you before that I'm in the paintings, except for two that belong to my family. The first one I made of my two children, and the other one when I'd lost my son and my mother and my husband. I never part with them. I took one of them over to Adelaide one time and cos they were right into art there — they stand up real critical, you know, 'What on earth is this? It's scary.'

It isn't quite finished. I could, you know, touch it up, but I mean who's to know that? You can change a painting any time you want to.

That's the best part. After I did it, I found at that house my nephew was very sick cos he got bashed. He was really very sick and I said, 'I'll leave these paintings here. They're spirits of the old people and they'll look after you.' He's as good as gold now. Nobody else can sleep in his room. They're scared of those paintings.

When you talk to artists like this, art critics, they're terrible. They make you see a side of you you've never known before. As far as I'm concerned art is the same as a funeral, it's a personal thing for me. But when I put it on paper, on canvas what I did, they were there telling me what I was going through and the moods I was in, and I thought, 'Oh God, I don't know that person.' But it was true, and it had to come from an art critic. Those colours do reflect on me too, that's a fact.

My son, Greg, and my daughter, Jennifer, they're very much into the idea of the moon controlling the spiritual world, but I don't see it as that. I see the spirits of course, and they can be my friends or they can be my enemies. But I know when to move along. I can sense those spirits and I'll get up. I got up from here at three o'clock in the morning, one o'clock in the morning, and went back up north. I just move along. I came down here last, three o'clock in the morning again.

Ground painting

I knew about this Aboriginal art they painted mostly on the ground, ground paintings. They painted about food. And it wasn't just the one person's effort. It was a little tribe or band of people. They'd all sit around and they'd mix up the emu oil with the mud and make it like a flat surface, and they'd all have their little bits and put it in, and they'd decorate it. If they wanted kangaroos, well they painted kangaroos. If they wanted something else they'd paint it. See they wouldn't put an emu and that in there because they want kangaroos. The wind carries it. But it was somebody else [Mick Little] who showed us that.

He had a bit of an exhibition and showed how it was done. He mixed up the emu oil and that sort of stuff. They'd decorate it with the emu feathers or stones, whatever they can do for such decoration. In '87 we went to Adelaide and Mick displayed his art and made a ground painting on the way to show what they do, and we photographed it. They reckon the wind carries that painting and leads you to it where the animal is.

Ceramic floor mosaic

Out there in Curtin University there's a mosaic in the Aboriginal section that I did. They wanted something, they showed us, in a circular thing. I said, 'Ah no worries.' There were three of us came out to do that painting. I was chuffed with that thing that you walk around, the circle. That was easy. You can look at it from anywhere that painting. Up above and you're looking down, or you're walking in, it's still the same. I suppose it was a bit cunning but it was good fun. I never wanted to sell them because all the paintings that I do I've donated, and there's some I won't sell.

I did that in '92 or '93. It was a competition to put in that circular foyer to say that all the Aborigines were coming together to study and learn you know. So I had a look at the diagram and it was circular. It didn't matter to me, because the way I was painting you see it from every angle around the painting. There were no squares. They weren't square paintings anyway so it was a breeze. I won that and I was happy for that because I'd been doing a lot of painting and tourists would come in.

> This painting is featured in mosaic tiles on the floor of the foyer at the Centre for Aboriginal Studies at Curtin University of Technology. The meaning is the coming together of Aboriginals to learn. They're followed by the spirits of their ancestors. We believe they keep us safe. The painting has shown our people coming from all parts of the country and from different tribes in peace. Aboriginals believe that if we can't walk together then we should always walk behind and support our leaders (Martin 2005).

I was really disappointed when they enlarged the painting to get the pieces the right colours or whatever. I thought, 'Gee, look where I've gone wrong here and gone wrong there!' But after a few years when you go back it looks really old. So that's why they didn't make it perfect. I was happy with that. It wasn't perfect anyway because the more perfect you are, the less black you are, that's my way of thinking, and the more white you are because they go for perfection but we don't.

Mabo

A lawyer bought this painting I did about Mabo. I painted it and he said, 'Oh I'd like to have that,' because he wanted to put it in Curtin.

8. Yarrna

Mabo

Inspiration for this painting came from the famous Eddie Mabo. Celebrations of Indigenous people across Australia happened immediately after the decision of the High Court of Australia to overturn the notion of Terra Nullius. At the time of this decision I was attending a national conference in Melbourne and watched Indigenous people from across our nation come together as a proud race. The feelings and emotions displayed at this time were electrifying, and through this I have painted the coming together of all Aboriginal people. I have illustrated Eddie Mabo as the centrepiece as a leader of our people, on either side his followers, and the spirits of his ancestors giving us strength to continue the struggle for Aboriginal land rights (Martin 2005).

He said, 'I want to give it to them.' So I said, 'Oh well, you know they might appreciate it,' and he paid me $2000, two and a half or something. When he went out I don't know what happened to it but I'll find out one day. It could still be there. Everyone used to go there and meet in his chambers, maybe from overseas and that, and they always looked at that painting and wanted to know more about it.

I went to a thing in Melbourne at that time. The Melbourne Aboriginals were going on and on. Everybody was shouting and dancing. It was electrifying. I didn't know what they were all squealing about first and I was really quiet. Then they told me and I understood it. So when I came back I painted that picture. He's the leader there, Eddie Mabo, and those people they stood behind him. That's always been the blackfeller's way. If you can't go with them you stay behind and you never walk away. Always walk behind. Never walk in front. If they don't want to walk with him, well, they stay behind.

Bush camps

There's an old one I did of the camps. There's a place out there in the bush where the blackfellers camped, hundreds of them, and all you could see was these bent over bushes. They're dead now, all dead. But at night time when you go into that area you don't hear a sound, and that's when they say the spirits take over. There are no bush noises, no nothing, not even a frog croaking or a cricket or anything. Everything there in that place it's untouched, but it's there. That's a big sacred site. You can't drive in there. You have to walk. It's scary. That's the one that he took, Mabo. When Mabo won they were asking for paintings to go into a competition and that. Mine didn't go, too late.

> This is one of the oldest paintings in my collection that tells of an old–old meeting place. This is a corroboree ground and a meeting place of hundreds of Yamatjis. Tribesmen from different tribes all over the country would gather, sometimes for a couple of weeks, and then they would disappear suddenly leaving all the camps behind. Now if you were to visit this place the remains of the camps can still be seen (if you know what to look for) but after sundown all forms of bush life will disappear. The old people say that is when the spirits of our ancestors take over. Not a bush sound can be heard anywhere. Everything is blanketed with an eerie, deathly silence until sunrise the following day (Martin 2005).

The half-caste girl

This one has been to Adelaide and back but I wouldn't sell it. This is the half-caste girl that's out from Cue. That's the Wadjari people's claim, but our Dreaming goes right to Cue. That's what this half-caste girl painted, the picture of a ship or a boat on the wall. Well that's just something like what I made of it.

8. Yarrna

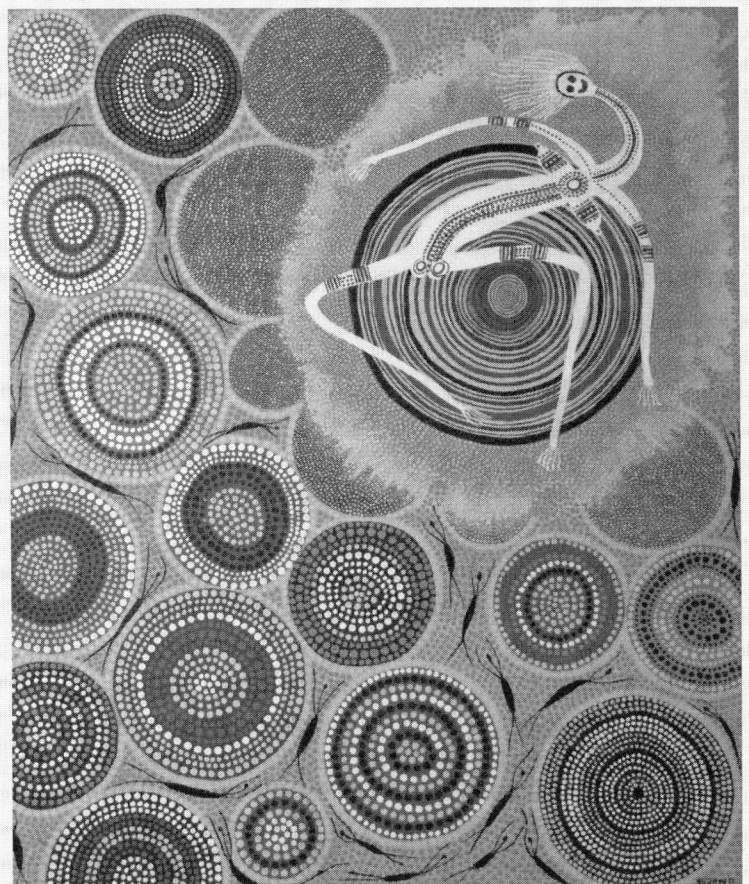

The half-caste girl

This painting depicts our Dreamtime Story from the Murchison. Hundreds of years ago a half caste girl with long blonde hair was born into the tribe. When she painted a picture of a ship on the cave walls the tribe knew she was someone special and could see into the future and past. She would perform in a special way and the tribe believed that some day she would return and save them. Each year or so the painting is touched up so that it never fades. I have painted my impression of the half caste girl and of the surrounding tribes that have the same belief (Martin 2005).

The seven sisters

This painting is just one version of the story of the seven sisters. Other tribes were out stealing. They'd wait till the hunters would go away and rush in to a camp and steal wives and things. One day they rushed in to get the coals of the fire the old fellers had invented or found — this is when everything was in darkness. So the old feller, the elder, put the fire out but he kept one coal, and that coal he took and he gave to his seven daughters. Apparently when the seven sisters were young people they went out hunting and they changed. They were the fastest runners of the tribe. He put them all on a big spear and he speared them up into the sky, but one fell off. One fell off so when you look at the constellation through a telescope there's only six you can see at first, and the other one's a little bit further away because she fell off the spear. That's why it's not really visible but it's there. The way I heard the story was the Man

The seven sisters

in the Moon always came after the Seven Sisters. That's what the stories are about, you know, people who don't do the right thing and they get made into the Dreaming.

The river of life and the inquisitive women

I call this one here [below] The River of Life. That's us, the people, kangaroos, emus, spirits, *bungarras,* turtles, whatever we ate. And these I call, not wandering women, they were like a sticky-beak it was, inquisitive women.

Girls through the law

I did another painting about girls being put through the law. You had the three elder women putting five young girls through the law. They were in the law camp [hand stencils], like a symbol of Aboriginality.

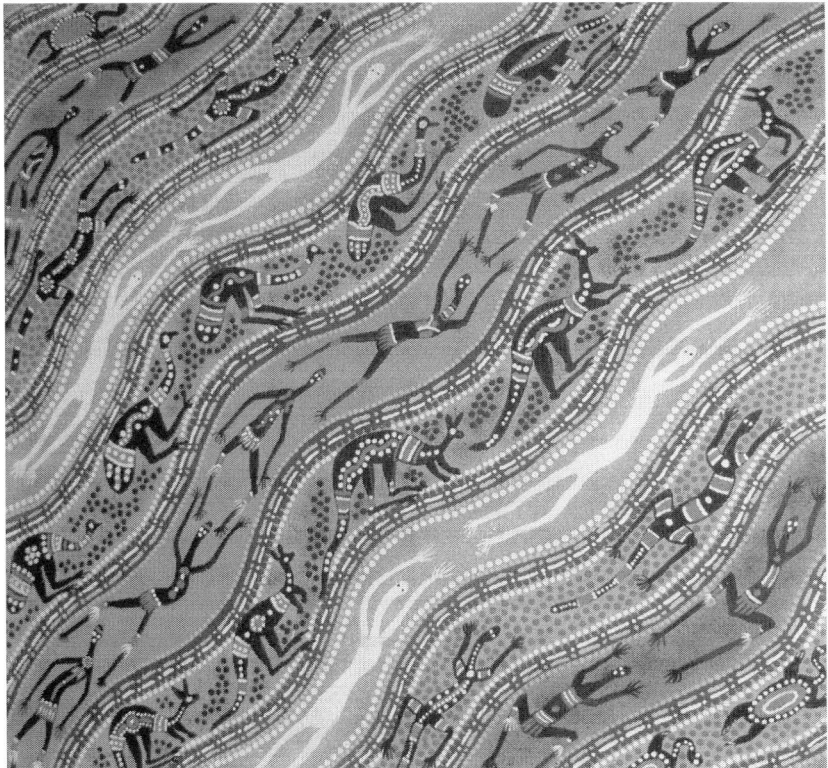

The river of life

I don't know why but I guess in my mind it's that they were tall skinny people. I can't help exaggerating the necks on them all. I suppose you might call it a trademark. I really love to draw those little women. When I did at first I called it Inquisitive Women.

Law men

I did one about law and Aboriginals and spirits too. You have that group of people to go through the law and to have a big law camp. They can take them from all these other places. But these are the law men, always got three. [Joan points to the three in the middle who are the law men.] There's one old law man, he's got two women there. They can always invite other people to go through the law at the same time, and that's where they get *ngalanggu* from. They call them *ngalanggu*. That means that they went through the law at the same time. They don't ever speak to that person again, and they give anything that that one wants to them, but they talk through a third person.

There's another version that shows only four tribes, but they come from everywhere. The people in it are elders that discuss what's going on and what's going to happen. It's another one about the meetings they have, and they all sit around in different places and they all talk. Probably discuss the next law camp and keeping up the law, what's happening in different tribes.

From the guts of the earth

This here just came to me one day, that these blackfellers were coming from the guts of the earth. When they say that Aboriginal law and Aboriginal people are dying out, the law's gone, it's not true. I mean you know whitefellers had Aboriginals saying the same thing.

Time

> This is my vision of long, long ago, of Aboriginals from a million years back. This painting shows that although people believe that Aboriginality is slowly disappearing, I believe that more and more of our laws and cultures are being practiced. The circles behind the figures mean that the Aboriginal culture is still coming forward but from the centre of the earth. The lines through the painting mean that, although a myriad of time has passed, our Aboriginality is as strong as ever (Martin 2005).

8. Yarrna

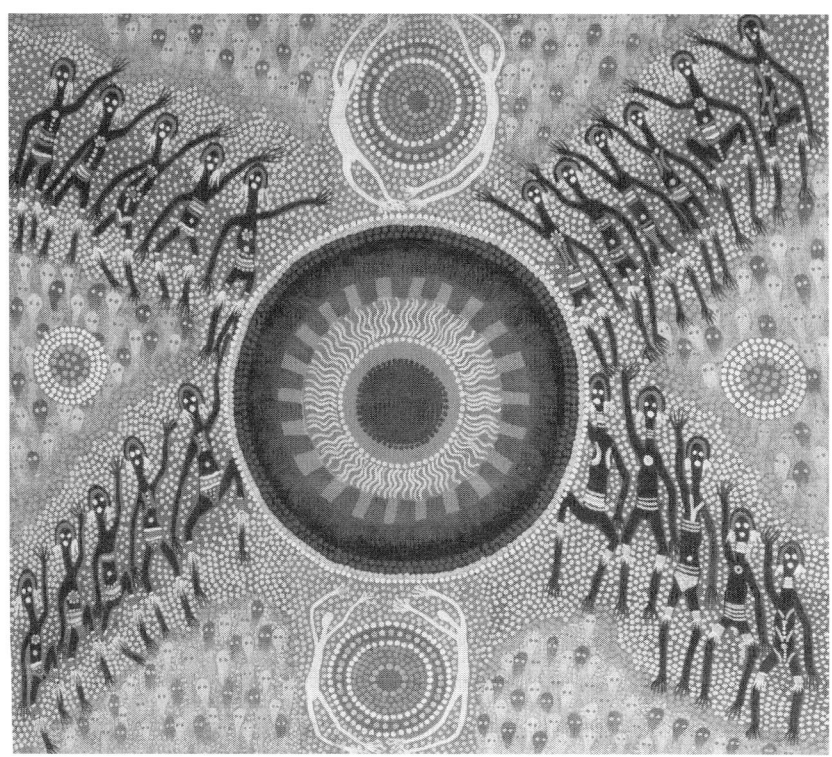

From the guts of the earth

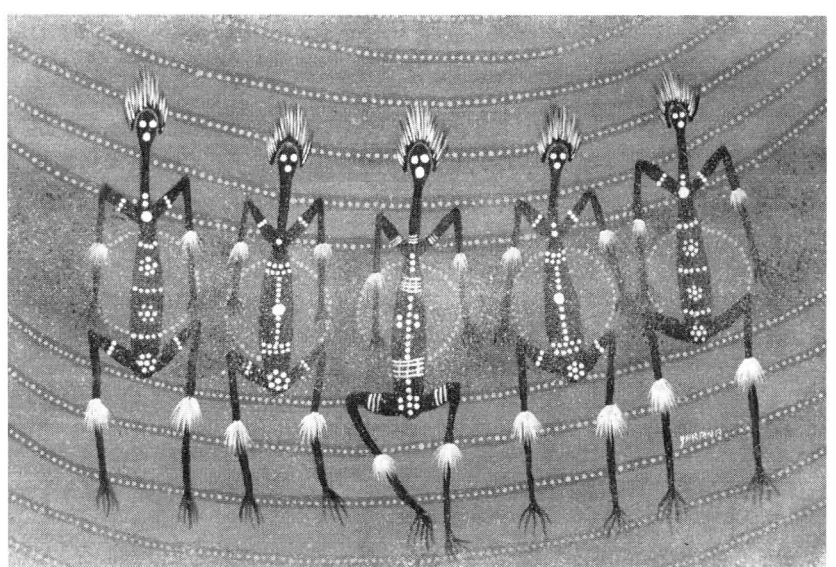

Time

Hunting kangaroo

This one's about the elders teaching the young ones how to hunt for kangaroo. The elders are painted in this picture, and of course we always got to have the spirits because those spirits keep Aboriginals alive, and the cycle keeps going on for the young people. Everybody's got to learn. The spirits, you've always got to have spirits. It's a spiritual world. They're just the blackfellers that track.

Hunting kangaroo

It is a well-known fact that the Aboriginal diet consists mainly of kangaroo. Men are shown how to kill and track kangaroos from when they are small children. Children are taught about the animal's habitats and natural instincts that they follow. This allows the tribesmen to hunt them with simple weapons with a great deal of success. In the Murchison, winter is the fattening period and during the summer months Aboriginals thrive off their meat as they are full of fat. This painting shows the learning time for the younger people (Martin 2005).

8. Yarrna

Hands reaching out

I sold this one when I was getting evicted. I thought I was slipping into a — like they were killing my spirit, so I put it on canvas. There were the fourteen hands that were reaching out to help me, my fourteen grandchildren at that time. And the Beemarra can be good or bad, but as I went there the spirit was lifting me up, came to get me and take me but not kill me. I wouldn't go into that bit. I sold it.

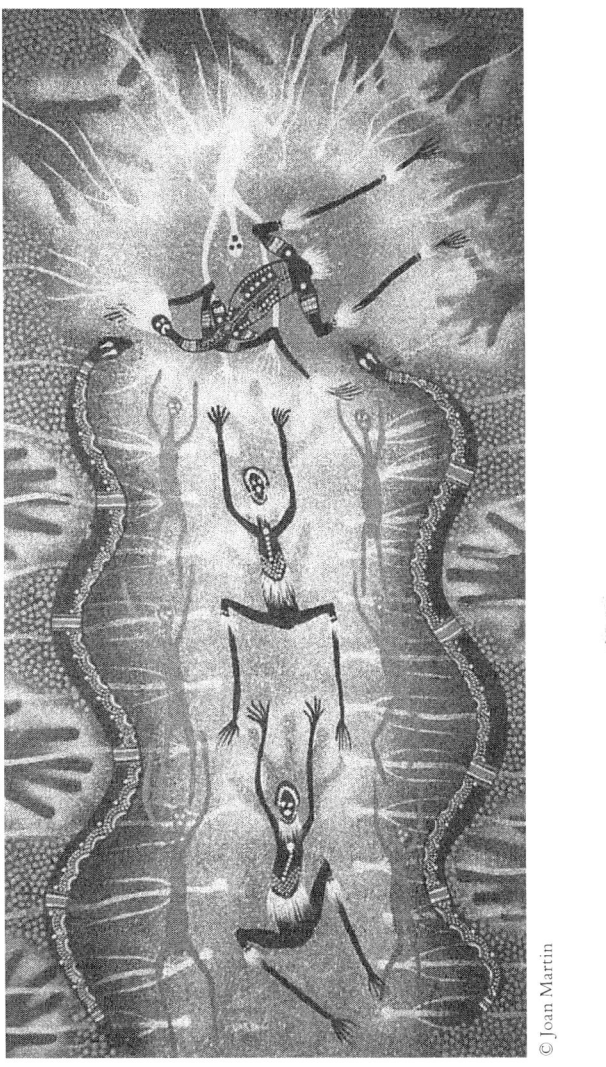

Hands reaching out

Emu and Turkey

I did one about the story of Emu and Turkey (refer p. 81). They were good mates but Emu was a very jealous person and one day she smashed up all but two of the Turkey's eggs. Turkey tricked Emu into burning off her wings. So that's how the emu lays a whole lot of eggs but can't fly, and the turkey only lays two eggs and can fly. It was revenge.

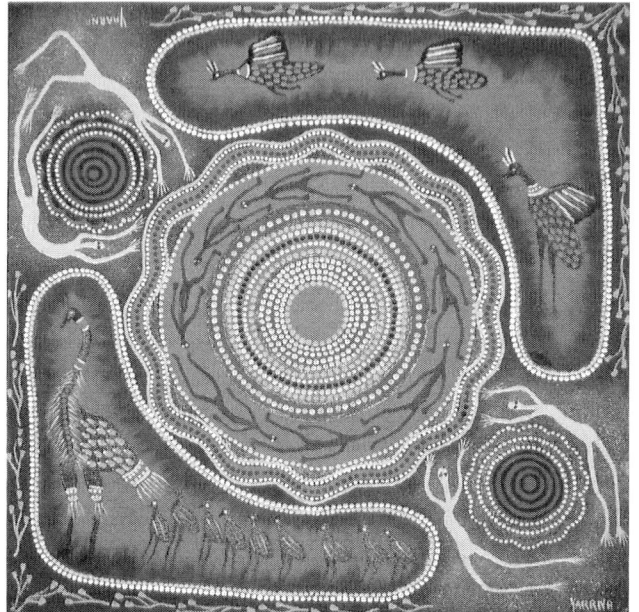

Emu and Turkey

Wudatjis

That's the *wudatjis* I was telling you about. I've got that version because they're little fat things you know, little short people. But I've also got straight up and down figures. They don't float around I don't think. I know they're around. They've got to be there, like those hobbits they found over there in Asia somewhere.

8. Yarrna

Wudatjis

This painting shows the *Wudatjis*. The *Wudatjis* can only be seen by the Aboriginal people and are short people similar to the pygmy race. They are known to haunt the hilly areas of the North West. *Wudatjis* are very hairy people and will show themselves only to certain people. They can be heard at night and most Aboriginal people have a fear of them. In the painting they are illustrated as floating, spirit-like. The centrepiece is the Elder, the protector of the tribe, keeping the *Wudatjis* at bay. Aboriginal people have a strong belief in their spirituality and the power of spirits. Spiritual figures are often shown in Aboriginal art as protectors from evil (Martin 2005).

Bush turkey

Bush turkey

There's a funny yarn about the bush turkey. They only have one partner. You can put them how you like. You don't have to draw them standing up or anything. Whatever is in your mind you put it on there, and while you're painting these things — and this is the truth — every time I do an Aboriginal painting I'm living in that time. I live that painting.

Bungarra

I had one I took to Adelaide years ago, in '88 I think, after the America's Cup anyway. That was '87 wasn't it? It's an old, old one. That's about the *bungarra*, the spirit of the *bungarra*. They always dig in the old rabbit burrows and they're there permanently, that's their home for life. It's like having your own home and your family come and they stay there forever. That's the holes where they camp. That's an old one.

The painting shows the mating of the Bungarra in the centrepiece and the Aboriginals are showing their respect, almost in awe, of this animal. On either side are the seasons which are illustrated in different colours and design: Autumn and Winter and Spring and Summer. Bungarra stay in the same burrow, nest for life and are known to come out and die above the burrow, never underground. The Bungarra can live to be very old indeed. Aboriginals' food custom is to hunt only as much as they can eat, never wasting food or killing unnecessarily (Martin 2005).

I've done similar stories but it goes deep down into the earth. It's just a different version of how I painted it.

Beemarra

The Beemarra can be friend or foe.

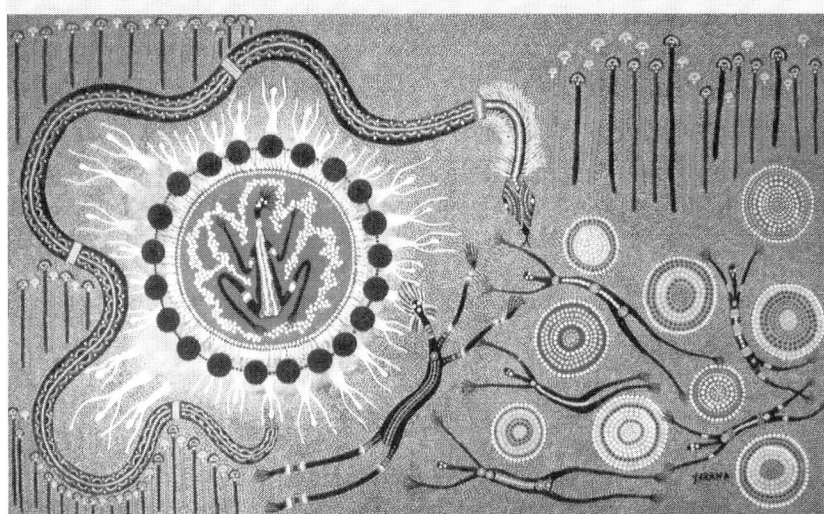

Beemarra

This is the water spirit which we call the Beemarra. It is the snake which is the keeper of our fresh water holes. The Beemarra is something similar to the Noongars' Wagyl. Most Aboriginals have their own belief from different areas and tribes. Our tribe is known as the Yamatji tribe and we come from the Murchison area. The children of our tribe are not allowed to go to the water hole before adults. Adults will throw a handful of sand into the water before taking water from the hole. This is a custom that is practiced throughout the Murchison (Martin 2005).

Emus

If you've ever watched an emu it gets up to all the different antics you like, any time. He plays. He jumps up and he goes down and he lays on his back and sticky-beaks. Stands. It's just the things they do.

I don't know what our totem is but I've always been inclined to draw emus. The emu's got his knee at the back of his leg, not on the front. It's quite funny. That's where the knee part is.

Emus

These are the Emus from the Dreamtime. To the Aboriginals they are magnificent animals. They are playful, inquisitive and friendly, besides being a part of our diet. I see these birds in a playful mood and have painted them in their many stances. Some dance inquisitively and some are just exploring or eating. In the background are droppings, and the circles are the camping grounds. Emus always lay their eggs and make their nests within five kilometres of the last nest, but within the same area. In the Murchison, the emu starts nesting after the first rain and the green grass has come through, usually after the cyclone season (Martin 2005).

9.
'Since ever the white man came'

When you look at it, they bring the alcohol, they bring the drugs, they bring their diseases, they bring everything. The vice, the corruption, the terrible things that are happening, you know, the paedophiles and the pornography and everything like that. Show me one blackfeller that knew how to pass that around. They never even got involved in that sort of thing. But it's like I was telling you that story:

> Our men now ape the white man's ways,
> And our daughters are things of shame.
> Thrown in the dust by the combo lust
> Since ever the white man came.

[A search at AIATSIS* identified the poem as *The Wonggi's Lament* by John Carins (1977). Although Joan's remembrance of the poem is not exact, it is important to highlight her understanding of it.]

I saw the poem many, many, many years ago when I was about eighteen. I think it was in the *Kalgoorlie Miner*. It was a huge poem. But that was the chorus, and it told all the stories about Aboriginal people and whatever done. It must have been a clever whitefeller who wrote it. It was just called *Since Ever the White Man Came*. But it stuck there and I never ever forgot. I had it, read it, and listened to it. *Kalgoorlie Miner* or 'Leonora Rag' or something, that's where it was. It's one poem I'll never forget cos it was so true. I wrote a few poems in my time. Don't know if I've still got them. Very dramatic talking, dramatising. When I get talking about things I get wrapped in them. Sounds really dramatic. I like pushing a point across.

Eviction

When they burnt me out over in Paris Way a whole lot of the paintings were destroyed. I had a couple left and they got destroyed as well. That's when I was renting a house at 39 Paris Way. I was evicted from there because they didn't like the government or something. I was used anyway, so what's the difference? It didn't matter to me. I tell you I don't regret anything, only that I haven't got a house. They didn't have any complaint against me. That was the worst part. No single complaints. The only way they could do it was through the kids. I mean they had stupid things like kids playing in the park unsupervised. Now what sane person would have to go and sit down and supervise them throwing a ball or playing cricket? We never grew up like that. It's only since you came to Perth that you learn fear, cos that fear was implanted through the murders and child molesters and everything else that they brought into this country. There was no fear in the bush. The only thing you could fear was the old people's spirits, and that's always there.

We had nothing except a little skinny mattress after that, me and my daughter Jenny. All we had was this little skinny mattress that I had, and she laid her doona down for her and the kids. We had about three doonas between us. Freezing. This was in Medina, Kwinana. We had nothing. Everything we had was gone, all the furniture, all the paperwork. They evicted Jenny and of course they took even my blooming big freezer and papers and photos, everything to Centrecare*. We never saw them since. That's three years ago [from 2006] and all that time after I've been living in a car.

It's disheartening. I mean we get kicked in the guts every day of the week. One day the police came. They saw Greg and the boys out the front so they pulled up and asked for somebody. I don't know names anyway. But it's an excuse to put us down and keep that constant, you know, 'I'm watching you. You don't do the right thing, you're finished.'

When I lost my son [Dean] he was thirty-six and it was the worst thing that ever happened to me. We weren't a big family and we didn't have many deaths in the family. My old Dad in Mount Magnet died first. Then my real father died, and my aunty and my Mum. When it started on my son well, God that was terrible. I never ever got over it. I still don't get over it.

Anyway when we were down here I still learnt and learnt and learnt, and I put in for the Native Title things. I took on that Native Title business and I got evicted by Homeswest. That was a story you'd never believe. I've still got the papers. I wasn't allowed to see them at first but the lawyer and I went to court. He was a government Crown lawyer, fighting the Crown. The first court was a good court. I still got evicted but it was fairer. I appealed against it and went to another court [WA Supreme Court] and lost. It was like, 'Stay in your place, little black woman,' you know? 'Don't you dare talk back to people,' you know? But anyway, I actually won that first court but it wasn't right for anybody to beat the government.

I know I beat it because they tried to make me say things. I'd never been to court for things like that but the blooming magistrate sat on the bench and she said, 'Don't you tell me you've never been to court before.' 'Well,' I said, 'did you want me to lie?' 'No you know too much about it.' What was happening, [the judge kept asking], 'Could they do this? These children.' That's my grandchildren. 'Could they do this? Do you think they'd do that?' I said, 'No. I told you I wasn't there,' when this happened and that happened, different things. 'But could it have happened?' I said, 'If I was in the criminal court as a witness for a murder or something my evidence wouldn't go. I couldn't even pass an opinion on it.' So I said, 'I'm not prepared to say yes or no.' They kept badgering me and at one stage I'd say, 'No, it didn't happen cos I know the kids wouldn't do it.'

It was a big case. The strategy they used those days — and that's ten years ago — they still use today. In fact they used it on my daughter [Jennifer] three or four years ago. Same strategies you know. Every government office uses strategies to justify what they do. Well in Homeswest they had an Aboriginal side of it, but they weren't the bosses. The white people were the bosses. They had a black face to put their word in for this and that, but not very often they had any say. And if you ask for a transfer they would find ways to evict you. They came around to the house. There was never anything bad you know wanted repairing, but they shifted me around the next street [to 39 Paris Way]. So now I'm still homeless.

Well in that street they were real anti-Aboriginal people from South Africa. There were 80,000 South Africans came during that time I was getting evicted. A book was written all about the South Africans all over Perth. But it ended up there was salt and pepper, eighty percent of the South Africans [that immigrated to Perth] came to Karrinyup where I was living. A South African lady went from house to house and she wrote in her reports, 'These people should not be living where we are,' like she was talking in South Africa. She was good friends with a minister. She used to meet with him constantly, sometimes just on personal visits. So that put you into an anti-social, anti-Aboriginal position straight away. If they're prejudiced people they start working on you.

I wasn't to know this until after. They didn't tell me the full strength of the eviction and how it came about. I never really did anything wrong. I never argued with anybody or imposed on them in any way. I never knocked on their doors and asked for help of any sort. I kept to myself and if they came face to face with me well I'd speak, but apart from that I never ever tried to be over-friendly with them.

Anyway they found a way. They started on the kids. Actually first Homeswest went out to Jenny's house, she was living in Heathridge. The woman said, 'Oh, I've got an eviction notice for you.' Jenny said, 'What?' The woman said, 'Oh Section 64.' Well Section 64 means that they could evict you for no reason. You have to go. She came round to Jenny at six o'clock. That was late at night after work. Anyway we got an advocate onto it and he took it around personally. He was working in Mirrabooka. He came back and he said, 'Oh well if you can stay with your mother for a while we'll get you a house within six weeks. You know we won't say anything about overcrowding or anything.' So I said, 'All right.'

The next step they took was with my son Dean. He put in for a transfer cos the house was too small. He was very sick at the time too. Instead of a transfer they evicted him. He couldn't get over it and neither could I. They didn't give him time to have anybody help him. They gave him twenty minutes to get out of the house in Karrinyup [Bridgewater Crescent]. They were going to change the locks. So he shifted everything out to the front lawn. I was in town and by the time I got there they were sitting on the old lounges out the front, him and his wife and six kids. This is what I'm telling you about the strategies they used. Well he shifted down to me with his six little kids. That was all right cos I had a back verandah. They sort of moved in there.

Then came Nicky. She was living there too [Karrinyup] and they decided to evict her. But in that same street [Bridgewater Crescent] they had five Aboriginal people at different places living and the street was only about 500 metres long. It was only a small street. I don't know whether it was even that. It might have been two or three hundred. But this lady that did all the petitioning lived in the street too and she went to work real bad, 'These people should not be allowed. And Dean Martin,' she said, 'walked past my house at least five times today. He's a known criminal with a bad record. He shouldn't be allowed on the street,' things like that. I was devastated when I read the complaints they put in and how they did it. [Joan also took in Nicky after she was evicted.]

So then it was my turn and they finally got us out of Karrinyup. I went to stay with my son Errol but we couldn't all stay there, and every place I went to we had to get out. My uncle and brother and that, they'd have kicked Jenny and her kids out, expected me to stay and I said, 'No, I can't let them walk.' So we went and we squatted in a house out in Midland. We found the owner was in jail and he wrote a note and he said it was all right. It was just a dump. Oh it must have been in its time a really lovely house, but it had squatters and they were burning papers inside and the ceiling and everything was burnt black, and graffiti. There was no gas. There was no electricity, just an old wood stove. So I was in Midland. I'd just go right out to Toodyay Road and collect wood for the fire. The doors weren't even on the hinges in the house and we'd hold the door up with cement slabs. We didn't have to pay rent cos we were squatting anyway. My youngest brother came and helped. But it was like everywhere we went there'd be a fire inside and outside the house. I couldn't work it out. Nobody ever worked out what it was, but I had my own ideas.

Anyway, six years ago when we shifted from that house to Glen Forrest [where they were squatting], two granddaughters were in an accident in 2001. I know I've jumped a lot of years but I wanted to tell you about it. One granddaughter got killed and the other one's wheelchair bound, at fourteen and fifteen. The police chased them, and they kept chasing them. Our lawyer won the court case when they had the inquest. He was a good lawyer. Actually I think he's a barrister now. He worked out the strategies and the timing and how fast they were travelling you know. The police chased them over the two-way and they were only two girls. They were aware of that and the lawyer said, 'Well, why did you chase them when you knew they were only girls?' He said, 'If they were eighteen and nineteen would you have chased them?' He said, 'I'd have chased them right to the end.' 'But isn't that what you did?' and he said, 'Yes,' because they were driving in a stolen car or something.

But I couldn't take the blooming court. That was the worst thing to ever go to. It's an inquest where you've got witnesses sitting in there listening to everybody else. The coroner makes the decisions. I was just so boiled up with her. She was putting words into the mouth of the police. See the one in the wheelchair came out and told them everything straight off first, everything as straight as a die. But because she had head injuries they tried to say she had a little bit of brain damage. She said, 'There's nothing wrong with my brain. I can remember everything.' She spent three or four months, actually I think it was a bit more, in Shenton Park Hospital.

It was a terrible thing. The first one we lost was a granddaughter. She was only six weeks old. That was a cot death. Then my son died at thirty-six. Then my granddaughter died in an accident. My brother died. It keeps recurring you know, even now. This is what happened to us because we were homeless. We're all still homeless. We don't know whether we can stay here or not [likely at Balcatta], me and my daughter that helps me. Homeswest won't give me a house because I went to court with them. Eventually they went to the High Court.

There was a lot of heartache. I cried for days. I couldn't cry in front of my kids and all the grandchildren. I had to make a stand, even when I was going to court in the tribunal. My son Greg was afraid for me. He said, 'No Mum, walk behind me. Don't let them take photos of you swearing and carrying on.' I said, 'Just hold your chin up, and your chest out. We're as good as them,' and he never forgot it. He tells his own kids to do that. But you know, we have had a terrible part of our life, and that's been in the last ten years. We had hard times before but nothing like the last ten years. People that haven't seen it would never know.

I still get lots of little things, comments, about how I live my life and I say well, 'You know what? You've never lost any children. You've never been as far as I've been in courts, and heartaches, and trouble with the police, and homelessness.' I said, 'Try walking in my shoes for a day. You'll soon get tired.' But it always comes up. It just got to me today. That's why I brought it out. I was just feeling a little bit depressed when you came and that's how this part of it came out.

Where are they going to put us? Cos we're no good here. We can't buy these houses. We can't live in a place where there's no money and food. The people that changed the workplace thing, they can hire us to say they did it, and sack us any time they like without paying us a cent. We're still on the streets; we're beggars for somewhere to go. In the end they can put us all on an island and blow us up so there's no more blackfellers. That's how simple it is. That's where they're heading. There's nowhere for us to go is there? They're in denial that we ever existed, to evict us from homes and push us out of where we are to live in this bush and streets. You know, after they've introduced us to society, and the food that we eat is European.

I'm on a wait term basis [with Homeswest]. After 2004 I put a request for a house in. It's now 2007, so I've been homeless since 1997. They're allowed to play with people's lives and yet they're so concerned about children. I mean you're not allowed to smoke in your own car now they're going on with, and they take the motherhood away from the women. They put them to work. They wonder why the prisons are full. It's because the kids don't have a mother and father. Both parents work. I mean, a lot of terrible things are happening out there.

Kim Hames was the Minister for Housing when I got evicted ten or eleven years ago. I reckon he tried to make up for it through Ron. Ron was using his consultancy. He took it over later. I was really mad at Kim Hames and I wouldn't forgive him. Anyway I ended up talking to him. He was very nice, apologetic. He sent me letters. Also stated in the letters, for whoever wanted to know, that he had no problem with me. I didn't have one complaint made against me, it was all aimed at the kids. They used the kids to evict me. They do this constantly. They put you in an anti-Aboriginal street and they let the neighbours do the rest of it. And then when you're shifted out they [the neighbours] move out anyway. They have no intentions of living there. It's just a tactic that's gone stale, really stale.

Living in a car

I suffer from a lot of stress being alone and homeless as well. This has bunged right up to my blooming shoulder. It's still swollen after a week. I come out in a big rash, allergic. But anyway it's over now, the rash and all. But I've had other problems. We're homeless and living in a shed, which kills me. I think I nearly died last night it was so bad. No heater. That was like sleeping in an icy cold cave. It was just unbelievable.

The shed is my grandson's. Believe me it's a wicked place to sleep. I've never felt so cold. There's a power point but what are you going to plug into it? You can plug in a heater but when you're in an old house or living in an old property the electricity doesn't run good, I can tell you. It just goes sky high. Bloody cost too much to run, heaters and things.

And it's equally hot in that shed as it is cold. It goes from one extreme to the other. Oh wicked. I spent last winter in a caravan. I think it must be the only house in Perth that doesn't have a bituminised driveway, it's still sand. It's just unbelievable. Mud here in Balga. When you're living in a clay pan, oh it's crazy. I can't handle it. I spent last winter in the cold in that caravan, and I was also down in Fremantle. I tell you what, the Fremantle doctor didn't pity me either. But I've been homeless for a long time. I won't beg. Mining companies might come up with something but I don't know. If they don't, they don't. That's just the way it is. But I'm not about to beg them.

I have very little to do with my family. I don't impose on them. I don't visit them. If they don't want to visit me well that's fine, because I just mind my own business. I think it's like everybody — that once your mother and father have passed away you take your turn as being the head of the family, and all you can be concerned about is your direct family. That's the way it is with my children.

I don't get out of the car much. I can only walk from the car to the house. Very short breath down here, but up there in the bush it's marvellous the difference. I can't walk much but I don't have the problems with breathing and don't cough all the time, and generally my whole body is a lot more healthy. I tell you now, I'd be there living if there was a doctor. There are no doctors and that's dangerous in my case, because I got heart problems and diabetes and thyroid that sticks out a million miles. You know that's just hopeless.

It was a good break, but it wasn't that good a break because I had problems. This young girl Jenny that comes with me and tries to help me — oh not young kid you know, thirties — she said, 'I don't know how you ever do it. How could you do it?' I said, 'I don't know myself but I just keep going. Something always comes out.' I'm a believer. But I'm also a blooming survivor. I don't believe that I'm just going to lay down and die because I'm cold. I went away and got a blooming heater. Cost the earth. But you know we chucked in. Patio heater, that gas thing. They are two hundred dollars, a dollar off. Well I don't want to run anybody else's gas bill up either, but I mean you'd only need to heat it early in the morning. Early when it's cold, and at night. You wouldn't want it on all night, you'd choke I found. I got to have fresh air.

I've got quite a bit of blankets I've kept through the times, and urns and things, old but handy. But in that shed we have four blankets on top. I put my little grandson on the foot end of my bed because he sleeps warm. He moved in with me, well he had four of those woolly blankets. You know not woolly but that latest way they've got. But I was crying with the cold this morning. Absolutely. My grandson got up and made a cup of Milo for me, and somebody lent me a heater, but they forgot to turn it on. Oh I said, 'What the hell's wrong with that thing? What on earth's wrong with it? There's no heat.' And they said, 'Well it goes straight up in the air.' I said, 'What's good about it in the air?' The bars weren't even on.

Sometimes I sleep in the house, but not very often because I feel safer in the car. It's always my safety. I've got heaps to do. You pack all this rubbish up and take it and, you know unpack my gear and get my cameras and my blooming films and, oh it's crazy. I've got heaps of things. I'm just homeless and I can't find them half the time and there's a pile in the car now.

I've battled all my life, every inch of the way. I had children that I love dearly but at the end of the day you know they live their own lives and they don't care what happens to you. I think the more you try to help them the more they want to take off you. I lost my house through that. Most of the time I sleep in the car, me and my grandson, cos I don't like to put other people out of their ways of living and what they do and things like that. It's not my way. I would much rather get out of their way.

My son Errol's only got a two-bedroom place and he's got his son there. So really there's no room for us. We're right though. We have a good sleep. Good rest. Sometimes I don't if I'm crook, but the risk you take eh? I used to camp over there at Shirley's [Joan's sister] in the driveway but I was afraid of that place, too eerie. We used to see little things, them little fellers, little *wudatjis*. Perth's unbelievable. You'd sort of feel them, and there'd be people walking through the gate every night, all night, yet nobody knew who it was. Used to feel the gate clicking, unclicking, then you'd wake up in the morning and the gate was open. It was weird. I'm just glad we're not there anymore.

I get really concerned about my little grandson. He's very lonely. He wanders around. I just about go off my head. You know it's just a thought that maybe they'll never come home. He's getting on to a teenager and they think they can explore anywhere and not get hurt. Lord I nearly died one night. I got a phone call from the police in Kardinya. We were living in Willagee. 'Are you missing four little boys?' I said, 'Oh God, what now?' But they had them at the disco there, were all the way down there, him and three mates, all around the same age, some younger. I was terrified but the mothers weren't. They just never turned an eyelash, and they still don't. I'll go for miles and look for him, here there and everywhere until I find him, but I see people that just don't care what happens and where they go. It's more than a problem. If they're talking about Halls Creek, they ought to get on to the women here, Aboriginal women and white who do the same things. They can't compare it because white kids have mostly been reared up to a better lifestyle. Put it that way. Aboriginals always had that same old careless attitude. But it's terrible since they became civilised. I think before that was much better.

My grandson Wesley plays up when I'm not there. I think he's very homesick for me more than anything. Rings me up, ten times this morning. He got suspended from school for fighting. He's twelve. It's the lifestyle he's had to live. He's only little for his age. I've got to go up and fix this boy up. I got to go for that boy because it's really important that he goes to school. I got to go and sign documents. That's the reason why I can't do anything else. He won't go to his mother. I want to go tomorrow so I can catch the school, so that I can sign it during school hours in the afternoon.

I've had Wesley since he was born you might as well say, a week and a half old and he's thirteen this year. It's a very hard thing to do. He's got ADHD* and I only realised by listening to the blooming wireless. I still say wireless when everyone else says radio. People came up with the things I've experienced with him but before I heard that people'd just say, 'Eh, just a spoiled brat.' They've got Wesley going to school at Geraldton now but they've given him big tablets and he's changing, and little things worry him. He's a very sensitive kid. It's just changed you know, everything changed when he went on to his tablets. He's quite popular at school and the teachers like him.

Illness

When I first went to hospital in Fremantle I had no idea I was so sick. I knew I was sick but I didn't believe I was that sick. So I spent five days in hospital and I thought I was right. I came out and I went to the bush and I was really sick. A million things went through my body while I was sick. The antibiotics had a terrible fight with my system. I can't get over it. I wasn't allergic to it. It was like something I've never known before. I've never been sick like that before. Never. It was a fight. That's what it was. The only way I can describe it is that the antibiotics were fighting the bad what was in my body. I had top to toe pain that I couldn't explain. And I had sores, sugar sores all over my body. I couldn't get them to heal. But after I had the antibiotics and that they went away and I couldn't believe it, just disappeared.

My body changed my life completely, even my way of thinking. I used to call for my mother to help me. This is how uncanny it was. I was sort of delirious. I went down the shop with my daughter and said, 'Come on. Hurry up. Mum's home waiting.' But she looked at me and I was so tired and sick I laid in the car, and I remember waking myself up and saying to her, 'Is Mum still there?' And she said, 'You know, there's something wrong with you.' I can just remember it so plain. I avoided that house [her son Dean's house]. I wouldn't go there. And when I went there to sleep and stayed that night, I had to ring an ambulance for myself to go to hospital. I knew my mother was there somehow. I seldom stay in hospital you know. I wouldn't have normally. I was saving all sorts of things, like bread and butter. 'Oh, what the heck am I doing?' I was saying to Nicky, 'They'd better not eat all that bread and butter because Mum likes it too,' and little things like that. I knew what was coming out of my mouth but I didn't know why.

I used to stay in Perth then and I knew where she was. The connection was so real, unbelievably real, so nobody can tell me there's no spirit. This is a spiritual world. I would prefer to believe in the Holy Spirit than not to believe in things you can't see or don't make contact with you. That spiritual world is something I've lived with all my life.

I could have laser treatment but what do I do? Where do I leave my car and my grandson who depends on me? It was holidays when I went to hospital and he stayed with my son. But his mother's there and he doesn't stay with her.

I've got some sort of growth inside that's causing me a lot of trouble. I don't want to talk about it. I don't want to think about it. But I know it's there. There's a goitre in my neck laying on the top of my aorta as well. My windpipe is like that [constricted]. I have lots of problems breathing. I have angina nearly every night. I can hardly walk and have a lot of trouble down the left side, and I have this big cramp in the stomach on the left side. It weighs my body down, can't walk straight. It's all in the stomach, and I guess when they take it out it will ease a lot of pressure. In the bush I'm happier and relaxed. That's the stress part though. It can't cure what's inside.

I don't remember what day is it half the time. I'm really not in a good way. And things come up and I move. I'm moving because I'm running from something and I don't know what it is. I keep running and running, I've got so many problems, family problems. Well the first one was, you might have read it in the paper, my grandson that these blokes attacked two days before Christmas last year. They're on charges and one was a footballer from Richmond.

I've got a short-term memory loss. Everything seems scrubbed out of my mind for a while and then it comes back. I don't know what you call it, but it's through the depression and things I've been through. Some things I get baffled, and I still haven't got a home. And then my dear old friend now [Ron Parker], I feel so sad about it. He's been a friend for the last ten years, no worries. A real friend in more ways than one you know, he helped us. A kind and considerate person, and someone that knows Aboriginal people.

Back to the bush

I'd rather be up in the bush. I'd get afraid of the spiritual world in the bush too. Oh it was really scary. I don't think I could live there for a great deal of time. Everything came back to me when I was up there. I was getting visions. Visions and flashbacks of every part of that journey, cos only me and my daughter Jennifer went. Well she was pretty sick, her liver's buggered, and I said, 'You've got to come with me. I'm taking you back to where you come from.' See that was her father's country — not only her father's, it was ours really, but that's the Badimaia claim. She's the spitting image of her father. Every part of that way I've been on, camped around, and I could see people that's dead and gone in different places. It was uncanny. Right the way down to Mullewa and Geraldton. But when I got to Geraldton I was saying, 'See this place, see that place.' And she was just looking at me. She might have thought I was off, but I wasn't.

I saw so many things in that trip. They were the good things. I blocked the bad things because there were a terrible lot of tragedies. There are things that I wouldn't do now. When you get older you think, 'Gee, what'd you do that for? How could you do that?' I'd shake my head and think, 'Gee, where the heck was I? Was I dreaming, or did it really happen or, what did I do?' A lot of those terrible feelings come through me and they haunt me. But today I live in the past, so far in the past that I don't know whether it's in the past or what's happening to me.

I went to hospital the other day because I was sick and my nerves went on me. All the hurt that my family feel, I feel it first. It's racked me. I feel the strangeness, like I was this little girl in the wheelchair, my granddaughter, and she's as defiant as the rest, as if she was normal you know. But hurting real bad they would never show it, and I was something like that you know, I'd never show. Well I was taught, 'You don't have to show your feelings. You can hide them.' I was in Morawa the other day and I felt really sad thinking about my mother's struggle for survival. We had a hard time. My Mum had citizenship anyway.

I'm forever up the bush. I go up there two or three times a year on kid's holidays and things. But it's hard when you're rearing up your grandson. I take him on site clearances though. See we were taught how to track, how to hunt. It wasn't only the spear that killed a kangaroo or an emu or whatever. We had to track the porcupine, and if you didn't know that the porcupine's foot was put on back to front you'd be going in the wrong direction.

I left out something missing, a story that describes the feelings that went through me, and more descriptions of the places I've been. The beauty I saw in the country wasn't the same as anybody else's you know. What I saw was beautiful or wonderful. Not everybody agrees. I just made it on my own. I was a deep thinker. I thought of lots of things, and I never really spoke until I was sure of what I was going to speak about. But I was a pretty quick thinker. Ah I had some fun in my life I can tell you.

See it takes a long time. If you rush for it, it's like having a conversation, but the things that come out are things that you feel. If you don't feel anything when you can sit down and tell somebody about it it's uninteresting. The interest comes with the feeling. Well that's what I thought about when I read the chapters [given to her by Bruce for proofreading]. Like I said, 'Gee, this is a feeling the story.' It could be boring you know, but really it wasn't a boring life. It was full of events, I can tell you.

Bruce, you could print it if you like, but my life has fallen to pieces since my son died, and that's ten years ago. It's a terrible life that I'm living, and you got to promise me that you won't publish it till I die. I don't want it printed until I'm dead and gone. But later when the land claim goes to court I'll be happy. You got no idea what they're doing towards that. They're trying to kill my claim. I laughed. The lawyer came here yesterday, and the government's never helped us before, but since we got a lawyer they want to do things.

I'm just buggered. I'm buggered and I've got to go so far. There are so many things! But you can't even begin. I think about, 'Why did I leave that out?' and all those things you know. That's a hard job [transcribing]. It's much like painting. Put it all in place. I'd better let you go. If I keep talking you'll hear my voice in your ears from the next two weeks.

Appendix

The Homeswest incident

In 1996 Joan moved into a Homeswest house in Paris Way, Karrinyup. In December of that year she was served with an eviction notice. What followed was a protracted and public battle. As a consequence of these events, Joan remained homeless for ten years. Yet she had lived in Pascoe Street, one section of which is only a block from Paris Way and Bridgewater Crescent, for twenty years from 1976, evidently without incident. Steve Mickler sums up the events in these words:

> From May through July 1997 the media devoted considerable coverage to the eviction of an Aboriginal family from their government-leased house in Paris Way, in the Perth suburb of Karrinyup. In a protracted controversy, Homeswest (the WA State Housing Commission) sought to evict the family on grounds of anti-social behaviour, based mainly on complaints from some neighbours. The family resisted the eviction order and put their case (unsuccessfully) to remain in the house to the WA *Equal Opportunity Tribunal* (Mickler 1997).

Mickler's (1997) theme is that sensationalist press reportage violated the Journalists' Code of Ethics by not giving all essential facts, so that: 'public antipathy towards the family's case was encouraged'. He identifies a woman (likely the 'South African' of whom Joan speaks, see p. 133–34) who had campaigned two years earlier in 1995, to have Joan's family members evicted from two Bridgewater Crescent homes (daughter Nicky and son Dean), where the woman was also living. This was about 300 metres from Paris Way. With no other option open to them, Joan provided emergency housing to both of her children and their families, including six of Dean's children. Mickler (1997) weakens his case through an untidy presentation of his facts and the use of emotionally charged language. In his defence, the article appears to be rough notes from an internet 'Culture and Communication Reading

Room' at Murdoch University which Mickler had set up. The eviction policy of Homeswest and social principles relating to it are discussed more soberly in Beresford (2001).

At the time the eviction notice was served, those living at 39 Paris Way comprised: 'Joan Martin, Dean Martin Senior, Dean Martin Junior, Janelle Martin, Samantha Ugle, Baymis Ugle, Wesley Ugle, Michael Little (at times) and before Christmas, additionally, Lena Michael and David Martin, Rodney Martin, Josephine Martin and Melissa Martin' *(Equal Opportunity Tribunal* 1997: 50). In mid-June 1997 they comprised: 'Joan Martin, Samantha Ugle, Baymis Ugle, Wesley Ugle, Dean Martin Junior, Janelle Martin, Lena Michael and her four other children, Jennifer Martin and her five children, Nicola Martin (at times)' *(Equal Opportunity Tribunal* 1997: 50). This was emergency housing.

Quentin Beresford (201: 40) notes that in the 1990s there was 'a continual spate of eviction orders' being served, suggesting that this was an intentional policy of Homeswest. This appears to be supported by the fact that Joan's daughter Jennifer had been evicted from her home in Heathridge prior to the evictions of Dean and Nicola. The eviction notice was a Section 64, which meant that Homeswest was not obligated to offer a reason for the eviction. At the time, their advocate recommended that Joan take in Jennifer and her five children on an emergency basis, something which would later backfire. Joan fought Homeswest all the way to the Western Australian Supreme Court, who found in her favour, ruling that Joan had been the victim of indirect racial discrimination. Homeswest appealed this decision and it was later overturned.

The *Equal Opportunity Tribunal's Substituted Notice of Appeal* (1997) concerning Joan Martin's eviction from the Paris Way address is a balanced document, critical of some of the actions of Homeswest while having reservations about Joan's testimony:

> It seems to follow from a consideration of the Evictions Report, which represents a reasonably thorough analysis of contemporary practices, that there are certain ambiguities flowing from the dual role of Homeswest which are reflected in the various policy documents, but these ambiguities could affect any Homeswest tenancy. In other words, the evictions report suggest that there are certain shortcomings of a general kind which may have untoward effect. Close attention has been paid to the situation of Aboriginal tenants, but the

> Evictions Report does not say expressly that discriminatory practices are evident, although it points to factors which may affect Aboriginal tenants in particular and suggests that greater use could be made of Aboriginal support services (*Equal Opportunities Tribunal* 1997: 25).

The Tribunal's noting of 'factors which may affect Aboriginal tenants' are consistent with what Joan Martin says about her role in broader terms, where she states her responsibilities as a grandmother and elder caring for family members in need of assistance. Her caring brief is a present-day cultural imperative in Aboriginal society. However, while they acknowledge the 'cultural obligation' they are at the same time sceptical of the extent to which Joan responded to it:

> The evidence indicates that family ties are a powerful influence within Aboriginal communities but the Tribunal is not satisfied in the circumstances of this case that independently of her sense of responsibility as a mother, Mrs Martin was obliged to take in up to 16 members of her family in a comparatively small house irrespective of the consequences. She herself conceded that when matters settled down she didn't necessarily want her children and grandchildren constantly living on her doorstep or in close proximity, even though they might have domestic problems. In the Tribunal's view, the accommodation was provided by Mrs Martin principally as a mother, on a short-term basis in order to meet an emergency and does not fit within the formula prescribed by the Act (*Equal Opportunities Tribunal* 1997: 98).

This appears in the Tribunal's discussion under the sub-heading 'Indirect Discrimination Plea' (*Equal Opportunities Tribunal* 1997: 96). However, the short-term provision of assistance from someone who was not only a mother but also a grandmother is entirely consistent with the cultural obligation. It appears the Tribunal's author is close to contradicting himself/herself. That author must have had some awareness that the argument was tenuous, for the next paragraph begins with the disclaimer: 'Even if the Tribunal be wrong in the view just expressed, there are other matters that stand in the way of the claim' (*Equal Opportunities Tribunal* 1997: 96). That is, that relatively few claims are based on indirect discrimination and in such cases that there is more detailed evidence. The Tribunal's 'General Observations' (*Equal Opportunities Tribunal* 1997: 102) might be taken as ameliorating their earlier remarks. 'It is apparent,' they write, 'that the principal cause of her eviction was the overcrowding brought about by the troubled domestic circumstances of her children and that she has lost her home largely because she tried to assist them' (*Equal Opportunities Tribunal* 1997: 103).

The report acknowledges the 'acute distress and bouts of depression' experienced by Joan Martin over the matter, exacerbated by her son's death following the lodgement of the complaint. Joan's observations about this period of her life and her continuing ill health and depression confirm this. The Tribunal's major finding is that: 'those principally affected by overcrowding and the associated problems are Aboriginal tenants, and it is Aboriginal tenants who are more likely to be affected by close scrutiny' (*Equal Opportunities Tribunal* 1997: 104). The last point was conceded by a representative for Homeswest: '[T]he likelihood that evicted members of an Aboriginal family will find their way to other members of the family for shelter, and the possibility that disturbances will then occur due to the consequent overcrowding, the combination of these factors is likely to prejudice the tenancy of the family member at the end of the line' (*Equal Opportunities Tribunal* 1997: 104).

In 1997 Joan's son Dean passed away. With what one hopes was unintentional insensitivity, the eviction from Paris Way took place on the same day as the funeral. Mickler (1997) notes the intrusion on that day, 9 June, of an STW9 TV crew. Throughout the eviction process Joan and her family faced harassment both in person and through the media, as well as vandalism, death and bomb threats. Following the eviction Joan was forced to move repeatedly from one uncertain housing situation to another as she describes in Chapter 9.

In 2004 Joan applied to Homeswest for a home, then in 2008 she was offered a house in Geraldton. She had little time to enjoy it before she passed away a few months later.

Chronology

Because oral story telling is, by its nature difficult to follow at times due to backtracking, repetitions and so on, it is useful to include a Chronology. It helps to make sense of the story. In this instance it provides a concise summary of Joan's life and family history, as well as an opportunity to include additional material, such as an overview of prehistory and contact history of the Widi area. Native Welfare Department (NWD) files were made available by Joan Martin and by her son Errol during the final stages of proofreading. They are cited selectively with permission from Joan and the family.

Prehistory

Archaeological evidence of Aboriginal occupation in Widi country has to be inferred from what is known of adjoining regions, because little published material is available for the Mullewa area. Keeffe (1995: 33–35) reports the presence of rock paintings at 'inland locations', grinding stones, horse hoof cores, stone arrangements at Canna, and yellow and white ochre deposits at the Greenough River, the Irwin River and the Wooderarrung River. The Irwin River is a watercourse that reaches the coast between Port Denison and Dongara south of Geraldton. Pleistocene dates for the Silver Dollar site at Shark Bay, about 200 kilometres from Widi country, range from 18,730 +/- 600 years BP (Before the Present) to 25,230 +/- 480 BP (Flood 1995: 285).

W.D. Campbell (1913: 10–14) describes three archaeological sites in Widi country: (1) at Narandagy Spring on a tributary of the Lockier River, (2) between the Greenough River and Sandspring homestead, and (3) sites near the Bowes River. All are 'caves', that is, rock shelters with paintings on walls or ceilings and some with hearths that Campbell excavated. They probably include the sites mentioned by Keeffe. Campbell (1913: 10) does not try to estimate their age beyond saying unhelpfully that they have various ages. This region (hence these sites) is not mentioned in Flood (1995) or in Mulvaney and Kamminga (1999). The Narandagy site shows hand stencils and the outlines of a tobacco pipe and a woomera. Campbell's (1914: 13) trench discloses bones, possibly those of kangaroos, and quartz chips, though he does not assess whether the latter were man-made ('artificial') or natural. The Northampton site at Appertarra contains hand and woomera stencils and a kitchen midden. The Willow Gully site, Northampton, has a palimpsest of markings and drawings upon older stencils of weapons and hands in white ochre, including several boomerangs and emu footprints, while in the back of the cave is the drawing of a large snake, not a stencil says Campbell (1914:13). It would be difficult to make a snake stencil.

Contact history

The first European to enter the Western Australian wheat belt between Perth and Geraldton was A.C. Gregory, who saw coal deposits on the Irwin River. Gregory also found deposits of lead ore in 1848 on the banks of the Murchison (Bignell 1987: 462). In 1839, George Grey named the Irwin River after Major Frederick Chidley Irwin, who at the time was Commandant at the Swan River Settlement (Landgate 2007b). White settlers moved to the Geraldton area following Gregory's favourable reports, and Geraldton began as 'Gerald's Town', taking its name from the Governor of the time, Charles Fitzgerald (Bignell 1987: 462). The town was surveyed in 1849. In 1853, a convict depot was established there and, in the same year, an overland mail service to Perth. In 1879, the railway to Northampton was opened. By 1852, copper had been found at White Peak. After 1874, when the jetty was built, the town became a port for the district. In the 1960s, a cray fishing industry was established, exporting to the USA (Aplin, Foster & McKernan 1987: 464).

The district was opened for settlement through the 1887 Land Act. The Calvert expedition of 1896 started at Mullewa. In 1915 the rail-way to Perth was opened, and in 1961–1962, Western Mining built a private railway for the shipping of iron ore and pyrites from Tallering Peak, forty kilometres to the north-west, where it was exported through Geraldton (Aplin, Foster & McKernan 1987: 466–7). However, a railway from Mullewa to Geraldton was opened much earlier, in 1894. According to the Landgate (2007a) records this was the year in which the township was gazetted. Morawa, ninety kilometres south-east of Mullewa where Joan

Martin was born, was gazetted as a town site in 1913. Other small towns in the area were gazetted relatively late in settlement history include Mount Magnet in 1895, Perenjori and Koolanooka in 1916 (Landgate 2007a). Koolanooka is of significance to Joan Martin and her family.

> [it] was chosen as the site for a railway station on the Wongan Hills–Mullewa line when the government planned the line in 1913, and the name selected for the station was Bowgada, after the adjacent pastoral station. The name was changed to Koolanooka before the line opened in 1914, and Bowgada was used for the next station south ... Koolanooka is the Aboriginal name for nearby hills and a spring, first recorded by a surveyor in 1893. One source gives the meaning as 'hill of wild turkeys' (Landgate 2007a).

The railway siding of Canna received its name in 1914, after the alternatives of 'Pindawal/Pinndawa' and 'Yondong' were considered. It was not gazetted as a town site until 1928 (Landgate 2007a).

Pastoral leases were taken up in the Three Springs area during the 1860s, but it was not until 1895, when a section of the Midland Railway was opened there, that the government began to make land available. In 1908, a town site named at first Kadathinni was gazetted, but the local usage of Three Springs stuck, and in 1946 the name was changed back to Three Springs (Landgate 2007a).

Mingenew has an earlier history. It lies sixty kilometres west of Morawa on the Lockier River and nineteen kilometres from the Irwin River. The Irwin District was settled in the 1850s, its principal lease holders Samuel Pole Phillips and Edward Hamersley: 'One of the datum points for leases at this time was a "Mengenew Spring", now Mingenew Spring, and this name was first recorded in 1856. It is Aboriginal, and said to mean "place of many waters"' (Landgate 2007a). The town site was not gazetted until 1906, following private subdivision in 1891 by Samuel James Phillips (son of Samuel Pole Phillips), and government subdivision in 1906 (Landgate 2007a). Sites glossed with Aboriginal names such as 'place of many waters' may sometimes be fanciful attempts at nomenclature. Joan Martin believes that the name refers to an Ant Dreaming.

Aplin, Foster and McKernan (1987: 467) only hint at the Aboriginal history of the area. In their profile for Mullewa they refer briefly to 'racial unrest' in 1985. 'Aboriginal resistance', European punitive expeditions and the 'dispersal' of Aboriginal people in the Widi region is reported in Keeffe (1995: 2, 3, 12). As so often happened in those times, shepherds and ticket-of-leave men were frequently responsible for Aboriginal killings. Aboriginal people retaliated by ambushing and spearing shepherds. Hostilities and skirmishes between settlers and Widi people took place in the Kockatea Spring area south of Mullewa, and culminated with a public execution of five Aboriginal prisoners at Butterabby, four miles [6.4 km] to the west of Kockatea, for the killing of Thomas Bott, a ticket-of-leave convict (Keeffe 1995: 2, 3, 12). The hangings took place in January 1865 before an audience of Aboriginal people. The police punitive expedition searched this area and travelled northwards as far as the Greenough River. Keefe (1995: 9–10) cites a long account written in the *Inquirer & Commercial News* on 15th February 1865. The Resident Magistrate of Champion Bay, William Burges, had persuaded the Colonial Secretary to allow the hanging. This event and other punitive expeditions and isolated killings by settlers, led to the weakening of Widi resistance. Epidemics of influenza, measles and smallpox broke out in the Victoria District not long after. In 1869 measles devastated Indigenous people inland and, according to Wittenoom, on the Murchison further north (Keeffe 1995: 32, citing Wittenoom n.d.: 36).

Widi country

Widi country covers much of the northern-most sector of the South West Division ('Swanland') and its transition eastwards into the Saltlake Division ('Salinaland'). Swanland includes the Perth coastal plain, extending from the country north of Gingin, southwards to Cape Leeuwin, and the escarpment country further inland as far as the Bremer Bay locality on the south coast (Jutson 1950: 32). The South West is Noongar country. The Saltlake Division is part of the desert region in the margins of the arid zone, and is characterised by strings of lakes, interconnecting streambeds and waterholes that have continuing sacred significance for Aboriginal people (Horton 1994: 275). The Widi, as mapped by Tindale, lived traditionally.

> From between Lakes Monger and Moore north to Yuin, Talleringa Peak, and Nalbarra; west to Mullewa and Morawa (Morowa); east to Paynes Find and Wogarno, south of Mount

Magnet; at Yalgoo and upper Greenough River ... Northern hordes around Pingrove pushed south-west to Geraldton down the Irwin and Greenough rivers in early contact times. (Tindale 1974: 260)

Mullewa, Kockatea and other towns in a line south through Perenjori lie directly on Tindale's circumcision boundary, which is also the territorial boundary between the Widi to the east and the 'Amangu' to the west. The Widi are not discussed under that name in *The Encyclopaedia of Aboriginal Australia* (Howie-Willis 1994a: 45), but appear to have been subsumed under the broader term, Watjarri (Howie-Willis 1994b: 1162). Joan Martin maintains that the Amangu and the Widi are identical. As Joan points out, Tindale (1974: 239) refers to 'my sole [Amangu] informant'.

Joan Martin's life and times

c. 1851   Ginny of Irwin born, estimate based on police records giving her age as being around seventy-four when she died on 23 May 1925. She married Tom Phillips Senior.

c. 1875   Ullamara, also known as Tom Phillips Junior, is born, based on his estimated age of about fifty in 1925. Mother: Jenny Phillips [Ginny of Irwin]; father: Tom Phillips Senior. Later married Amy Cameron, their children are Janie, John, Reg, Frank, Tom, Eva (aka Mrs Norman Harris) and Irene.

c. 1886   Amy Cameron is born to Julia Cullawerri (fb), first wife of Amy's father, Charles Cameron (hc).

c. 1906   Horace Phillips is born. Mother: Amy Phillips (*née* Cameron); father: Tom Phillips Junior. He is later employed at Mount Phillip Station (NWD File 869/39).

c. 1910   Jane Phillips is born. Mother: Amy Phillips (*née* Cameron); father: Tom Phillips Junior.

c. 1915   Jane Phillips (Joan's mother) is born, based on an estimated age of twelve in 1927. Mother: Amy Phillips (*née* Cameron); Father: Tom Phillips Junior.

1916   John Phillips is born, based on estimate that he is eleven in 1927. Mother: Amy Phillips (*née* Cameron); father: Tom Phillips Junior.

Early 1920s   Jane Phillips is taken to Moore River Settlement.

1925	A note written on 4 February details Tom Phillips Junior as being employed by John Campbell of Little Mingenew, with a wage of £1 ($1.50) a week, as well as food for himself, his wife and children. Ginny of Irwin dies near Morawa on 23 May at approximately 74 years of age.
1928	Amy Phillips (*née* Cameron) dies 17 August at about 42 years of age at the Moore River Native Settlement (NWD File 54/27). Deputation to the state government with Norm Harris (*see* Haebich 1992: 273–4).
1933	Tom Phillips Junior dies of heart failure on 12 March 1933 (NWD File 54/27). Sister Kate's Children's Cottage Home is established (Haebich 1992: 318).
1934	Jane Phillips leaves the Moore River Native Settlement on 1 October (NWD File 54/27 & 298/32). John Phillips' recorded occupation is Police Tracker in Moora on 20 November (NWD File 54/27).
1935	John Phillips has been a Police Tracker for at least six months at Mount Magnet on 22 March. On 24 May, his liaison with Ethel Billabong results in twins, Rima and Leslie born; the twins die on 3 June. Another child, Eunice, is conceived at a later date (NWD File 54/27).
1936/37	Joan's older brother Bill Lewis is born. John Phillips ceases as a Tracker on 4 April.
1938	John Phillips marries on 3 May (NWD File 54/27).
1940	John Phillips fractures his forefinger on 8 October when working for Mr Thomson of Warren Point, Moora (NWD File 54/27).
1941	Joan Martin (*née* Phillips) is born in Morawa on 2 March. Mother: Jane Martin (*née* Phillips). Joan's children are Errol, Greg, Dean, Jenny, Nicola, Stephen and Sandra. Early memory of earth tremor when Joan is about ten months and Joan's older brother, Bill, is four or five years old.
1943	John Phillips' Certificate of Exemption from the provisions of the *Native Administration Act* is approved on 17 September by the Hon. Minister, for him, his wife and any of their children under 14 years of age. He is arrested

	for assault on 16 November and the Certificate cancelled on 10 December (NWD File 54/27).
1945	Joan's early memories of the end of the Second World War.
1946	Death of Charlie Cameron. Joan remembers Tindale passing through Morawa. Joan attended Morawa Primary School and remembers living near Koolanooka to avoid Welfare's unwelcome attentions. When Welfare catches up to them Joan's father and mother move to Perenjori, where her father gets a job on the railways. Joan stays in Morawa with an aunt and attends Morawa High School.
1952	Joan goes to Perth for first year and half of second year high school at Perth Modern School. She lives in a hostel (the Alvin House) for two years.
1954	Joan leaves school and returns to Morawa to live with her aunt, where she works on a farm for two or three weeks. She then works as a telephonist in the Morawa Post Office. Later Joan leaves her aunt's place and lives with cousins.
1956	Ruth Fink, an ethnomusicologist, visits Mullewa recording songs.
1958	Joan Martin marries Leonard Michael Martin (Lennie). Errol is born to Joan and Ron Simpson on 29 September.
1959	On 18 September, Joan and Lennie's son Gregory is born in Morawa. Joan's family moves to Mount Magnet.
1961	On 10 May, Joan and Lennie's son Dean is born in Mount Magnet.
1962	On 19 November, Joan and Lennie's daughter Jennifer is born at Mount Magnet. The family stay at the Mount Magnet reserve until Lennie buys a house. Joan takes her children into the bush surrounding Mount Magnet often over the years. The children go to Mount Magnet Primary and Geraldton High School. Joan returns to Mount Magnet. There were many floods in Mount Magnet over the years.
1967	On 19 September, Nicola (Nicky) is born to Joan and Kevin Cameron in Mount Magnet.
1969	On 15 December, Joan and Noel's son Stephen is born and given to a foster mother.

Chronology

1970	Joan stays in Mullewa with her Uncle Victor Harris, then with a cousin. She lives in government housing in Geraldton for three years to stay close to her sister Shirley. The family survive there on gambling and fishing. Jennifer falls sick.
1970/1971	Joan witnesses an initiation corroboree at Roebourne.
1971	On 28 March, daughter Sandra is born to Joan and Sid and is given to the same foster mother as Stephen. Not long after both children are fostered by Jim and Leonie Spring.
1974/1975	Lennie passes away. Joan moves to Ramsay Street, Karrinyup.
1976	Joan obtains a Homeswest house in Pascoe Street, Karrinyup where she lives for twenty years.
1977	William 'Bill' George Lewis (Joan's stepfather) dies on 23 August aged about seventy-seven.
1981	Joan's aunt (who moved to Perth thirty or forty years prior) dies.
1987	Art exhibition is put on by Michael (Mick) Little in Adelaide just after the America's Cup and Joan's painting career commences. Joan's mother, Jane Lewis (*née* Phillips), dies.
1992/3	Joan wins an art competition held by the Curtin University of Technology for the design of a ceramic floor mosaic at the Centre for Aboriginal Studies (CAS).
1993	Joan attends a women's conference in Melbourne.
1996	Joan moves to a Homeswest house in Paris Way, Karrinyup. In December she is served with an eviction notice which began a protracted and public battle. See Appendix: The Homeswest Incident for further information (p. 145–8).
1997	Death of Joan's son Dean. The eviction from Paris Way comes on 9 June, the same day as the funeral. Mickler (1997) notes the intrusion of an STW9 TV crew on the day. Joan spends between now and 2008 homeless.
2001	Joan shifts to a house in Glen Forrest. An inquest is held into the car crash death of her granddaughter Marjorie and the injury of another girl. There is also the cot death of another granddaughter.
2004	Joan applies to Homeswest for a home.

Chronology

2005	Joan compiles a commentary on selected items of her art to show connection to country in support of her Native Title claim, assisted by Ron Parker's sister Jeanette Mellor, a poet, writer, artist (Martin 2005).
2006	Joan's grandson has a dream about Tom Phillips Junior.
2007	On 10 August Joan's brother Bill passes away. Joan attends his funeral. On Friday, 28 December, Ronald T Parker, Director of Australian Interaction Consultants and a close friend and mentor to Joan, passes away.
2008	Ron Parker's funeral is held on Monday, 7 January. Joan is unable to attend. In April, Joan gains a Homeswest house in Geraldton. Reconciliation is effected between her and Kim Hames, the Minister for Housing. In August, Joan hears spirits crying between Morawa and Mullewa. Joan passes away on 6 October. The funeral is held in the Norfolk Chapel at Karrakatta Cemetery on 21 October. Kim Hames pays tribute to Joan at the memorial service. Joan's ashes are scattered at the Coalseam for the release of her spirit.

Glossary

ADHD	Attention Deficit Hyperactivity Disorder
AIATSIS	Australian Institute of Aboriginal and Torres Strait Islander Studies
AIC	Australian Interaction Consultants
Amangu	Language group mapped by Tindale as traditionally occupying the coastal area from Geraldton inland to Morawa. Joan Martin claims justifiably that Tindale was in error.
anthro	Anthropologist.
Badimaia	Language group mapped by Tindale as traditionally occupying an area adjoining Widi country to the north-east.
bardies	Edible wood grubs, *Bardistus cibarius* (Wilkes 1978: 17).
battler, battling	Person who struggles for a living: 'to work in low-paid employment' (Wilkes 1978: 23).
Beemarra	Also spelt 'Beemurrah'. The Rainbow Snake. In the northern Kimberley one of its names is Brimurer (Elkin 1977: 124).
biguda	Rock kangaroo.
blackfeller	An Aboriginal person whose parents are both Aboriginal, a distinction that is specific to the Kimberley area, but differs in regions across Australia (Morris 1972: 33). The word can have offensive connotations, but nowadays is often used in self-reference and as a badge of pride by Aboriginal persons whose parents are of a different ethnic background.

Glossary

bobtail	A lizard commonly found in most southern areas of Australia. Joan refers to them as a 'coastal land fish', a local metaphor that relates to the fact that bobtails have the same colour meat as a fish.
boggada	A type of seed. Joan believes a siding out from Morawa called Bowgada derives from this source.
boob	The cells at the Moore River Settlement, Mogumber.
boong	'An Australian Aboriginal; New Guinea native; any Asiatic: derogatory' (Wilkes 1978: 46).
bough shed	Flat roofed timber and bark shelter.
bungarra	Racehorse goanna.
bush telegraph	Rapid spreading of information, gossip or rumour. Source: 'Confederates of bushrangers who supply them with secret information of the movements of police' (Morris 1972: 72).
CALM	The former Western Australian Department of Conservation and Land Management, now the Department of Environment and Conservation.
carara	A curly and prickly bush, and also the name of the black and gold seeds that come from it. Bindon & Chadwick (1992: viii), claim that *cara-cara* means 'coastal bush containing *bardies*'. Joan associates the name with Karara Homestead east from Perenjori on the Rothsay Road because it has lots of *carara* bushes.
Centrecare	Organisation in Perth providing parent and adolescent counselling and mediation, domestic violence counselling, and accommodation for homeless families.
culyu	Large purple tuber like a sweet potato. Also spelt *cullyu*.
djinigubbies	Assassins similar to the featherfoot. So named because they are said to obscure their tracks by walking on wet ground, whereas the featherfoot is said to hide their tracks by wearing emu feather sandals (*ji-na, jinna, jeena* = foot; *gabbi*, etc. = water; Bindon & Chadwick 1992: 268, 431-432). Also spelt *djinagabi*.

djubbies	Small lizards.
djurrnda **stone**	A solid gold stone shaped like a mushroom that is said to rise out of Lake Monger. Joan's mother told her only special people can see it (see pp. 76–7). Possibly from the word *djundal* meaning white (Bindon & Chadwick 1992: 45).
Dreaming, Dreamtime	The ancestral creative period in which the present day physical and moral world was established, told through stories in which ancestors as different animals created the landforms.
Dreaming track(s)	Routes across the country taken by the Dreamtime ancestors and the landmarks they created on the way.
dunart	The little kangaroo mouse (*dun-nart* = tree mouse; Bindon & Chadwick 1992: 328, source: Isaacs 1949).
full-blood	Person whose parents are both Aboriginal. The term, nowadays regarded in some Aboriginal circles as insulting but in general use among other Aboriginal communities, is often indicated in old records as 'fb' or a variant of the initials. Cf. half-caste.
gumbara	'A small tomato bush, it usually grows across granites: little red tomatoes, wild tomatoes' (see pp. 69–70). Also known as *tumbara*.
genocide	'The definition of genocide adopted in the UN Convention, now the basis for international law, includes: "Killing members of the group; Causing serious bodily or mental harm to members of the group; Deliberately inflicting on the group conditions of life calculated to bring about its physical destruction in whole or in part; Imposing measures intended to prevent births within the group; Forcibly transferring children of the group to another group"' (Curthoys 2003: 196).

giddi-giddi	Powder used to sing people with. The term 'to sing' can have a number of meanings depending on the context. In some contexts it means calling death upon a person 'sing their death'. Joan uses the term to mean call someone or something to you, mentally or physically, sometimes using *giddi-giddi*.
gnamma holes	A type of hollow formed by wind and rain in rocks that collects water, found mostly in Western Australia's Sandland and Salinaland (Jutson 1950: 365). Bindon and Chadwick (1992: 58) describe *gnamer* as meaning rock hold, or *gnamnar* meaning 'water; standing in water'. It is a Noongar word according to one source (Dictionary.com n.d.).
half-caste	A person, one of whose parents is Aboriginal, and the other parent of a different race. Nowadays the term is regarded as offensive in most Aboriginal communities, while in some Aboriginal communities it is still in general use. The term is often indicated in old records as 'hc' or a variant of the initials. Cf. full-blood.
Joe Blake	Rhyming slang for snake (Wilkes: 1978: 189–190).
kagul	Crow. Also the nickname of Joan's son Greg (*karler* = crow, Northampton, Bindon & Chadwick 1992: 246).
kalla	Fire (Bindon & Chadwick 1992: 266).
Kalyudi	'I painted under two different names. Aboriginal people call me Kalyudi. That's the crow, a woman, Kalyudi, and I shortened it and called it Kalla, cos *kalla* means fire in our lingo' (see p. 113).
kooda	Similar to *knooda* meaning brother, elder (Bindon & Chadwick 1992: 227, source: Curr 1887). Joan uses it in reference to a nickname given to her husband Lennie (see p. 72).
Kuniya	Name of the Rainbow Snake in the Ernabella area. Cf. Beemarra, Wagyl.

lakes	There is a major salt lake running north-east to south-west within three kilometres of Morawa which Joan describes walking across in her youth. This is the first of the string of lakes that run south and is part of the Widi Dreaming track. It has a natural spring.
line cutters	'He was one of the line cutters — that's the English word — from sacred site to sacred site, and he'd have to look after them and check the country from one point to the other' (see pp. 56–7, 68).
lingo	Aboriginal language (in context, Widi).
maggawala	Hat. Joan takes issue with this spelling (see p. 50).
maluka	Chief, boss (Wilkes 1978: 212) or 'old man'. It is a term of respect.
mara	Hand.
marrloo	Red kangaroo.
mickey minor	A colloquial name for magpies in the Morawa district.
minga-minga	Ant, Ant Dreaming at Mingenew, *mun-gat, manyipp, mingebup, manyet* meaning ant in Noongar languages (Bindon & Chadwick 1992: 202–203).
moban	More often in the literature spelt *maban*, the term refers to a person who has magical powers, sometimes called a 'native doctor'; also the name given to the powers they have. It is in wide use throughout Western Australia, especially in the far north (the Pilbara and the Kimberley's), but is mentioned circumspectly.
Morawa	A town located in Western Australia. The name had been attached to a rock hole on maps of the area in 1910 and is thought to have 'possibly derived from "Morowa" or "Morowar", the Dalgite, a small marsupial which burrows into the earth. Another possible meaning is "the place where men are made"' (Landgate 2007a). Also known as *dal-gyte*, 'burrowing animal, size of the weasel' (Bindon & Chadwick 1992: 41).

Mullewa	A town located in Western Australia. The meaning of the Aboriginal word *mullewa* — first used in 1869 pastoral lease plans, and later by John Forrest in 1873 — is given in Landgate (2007a) as 'place of fog'. But Mullewa was named from the Aboriginal for 'swan' say Aplin, Foster and McKernan. Bindon and Chadwick (1992: 401–402), list variants of *marlee, mallee* for swan but none for 'fog', while *mallo* means devil or spirit for people 'north of New Norcia' (Bindon and Chadwick 1992: 100).
National Native Title Tribunal	A federal government agency set up to help people involved in the native title process.
ngalanggu	People who went through the law together and shared a special social relationship after that, which Joan describes in detail on pp. 34, 122.
ningari	A finch.
ninghan	Echidna or spiny anteater, also called porcupine.
nooka	'There's something in the 'nooka'. It's Aboriginal for 'water' I think. Yandanooka, Koolanooka, Merkanooka, there were heaps of them that meant something to do with water' (see p. 102). Also, *gnura* means 'water standing in a well' according to Bindon & Chadwick (1992: 432).
Noongar	An Aboriginal person from the south-west of Western Australia. Also spelt Nyungar and Nyoongar.
nyiawl	Mallee hens. They lay these pretty little pink eggs in a big mound, mallee hens (*naw, gnow, gnow-o* = mallee fowl; Bindon & Chadwick 1992: 318).
papertalk	A family name, Papertalk, also a name for someone who was a mailman. Cf 'paper yabber' (Wilkes 1978: 367).
porcupine	Echidna, spiny anteater, *ninghan*; often shortened to 'porkie'.

quandongs	'The quandongs come out during the summer and spring. People make jam from them now but those times they used to eat the seeds as well. Emus love them. They get them off the tree' (*quon-dan* = emu berry; Bindon & Chadwick 1992: 157).
rock up	Arrive.
shame	Damaged self esteem, embarrassing.
show, had a	In this context, 'he found some gold and had a show', meaning to have his mine set up (Wilkes 1978: 297). Also sometimes called 'a plant'.
skin	Colloquial expression (metaphor) referring to an Aboriginal naming system in which each person stands in a classificatory kin relationship with others. In the Kimberley there are eight matching female and male pairs, called by anthropologists the subsection system. In the desert areas such as that of the Widi, it is called the section system, consisting of four matching pairs. The choice of marriage partners is guided by this system.
snotty gobbles	Edible berries of the genus *Cordia*. '*Cordia* is a genus of shrubs and trees in the borage family, *Boraginaceae*. About 300 species have been identified worldwide, mostly in warmer regions … A number of the tropical species have edible fruits, known by a wide variety of names including clammy cherries, glue berries, sebesten, or snotty gobbles' (Wikipedia contributors 2011).
Tardun Mission	A boy's institution founded in 1948 under the Pallotines at Saint Joseph's Farm near Tardun (Biskup 1973: 2001).
Ullamara	Nickname for Tom Phillips Junior. Possibly meaning 'quick hand', from *ullar ullar* meaning speed, readiness, and *mara* meaning hand (Bindon & Chadwick 1992: 167, 281, source: Salvado 1977).
ute	Australian colloquialism for utility: 'vehicle combining the features of a sedan and a truck' (Wilkes 1978: 350). Americans call them 'pickups' or 'pickup trucks'.

wajela	White man. Otherwise referred to as *widgella* (Bindon & Chadwick 1992: 439).
Wageral	Tribal people of Narandagy.
walkabout	Meaning travelling about the country, relating to nomadic Aboriginal movement from place to place, usually within their language group country.
western grey	Coastal kangaroo.
whitefeller	European person, white Australian, *wajela*.
wicked	Painful, uncomfortable.
wilgi	Ochre.
Wogera	Locality on the Irwin River where Joan's mother was born, related to the local Wageral group.
Wongi	An Aboriginal person from the Western Australian Goldfields region. Also known as Wongathas.
wudatjis	Little people. Spirits in human (Aboriginal) form that frequent rocks and hills. They are known throughout the south-west among the Noongar people, and are sometimes associated with trees in swampy places.
yakkaiing, yakkai	To call out, shout.
yamatji	Friend in general terms.
Yamatji	An Aboriginal person from the Gascoyne region in Western Australia.
Yarrna	Joan's pseudonym as an artist. It appears on most of her paintings, because they tell a story: 'Yarrna, I stuck to that name. I just made it up because you're telling a good yarn' (see p. 113).

Bibliography

Aplin, Graeme, Foster, S.G. and McKernan, Michael 1987, *Australians: events and places,* Fairfax, Syme & Weldon Assocs, Broadway.

Attwood, Bain & Foster, S.G. (eds) 2003, *Frontier conflict: the Australian experience,* National Museum of Australia, Canberra.

Bates, Daisy 2004, *My natives and I: incorporating the Passing of the Aborigines: a lifetime spent among the natives of Australia,* ed. P.J. Bridge, Hesperian Press, Victoria Park.

Beresford, Quentin 2001, 'Homeswest versus Aborigines: housing discrimination in Western Australia', in Richard Davis 2001, *Australian Aboriginal Studies,* Australian Institute of Aboriginal and Torres Strait Islander Studies, Canberra, Issue 2, pp. 40–6.

Bignell, Merle 1987, 'The wheatbelt and central coast', in Graeme Aplin, S.G. Foster & Michael McKernan, *Australians: events and places,* Fairfax, Syme & Weldon Assocs, Broadway, pp. 462–463.

Bindon, Peter & Chadwick, Ross 1992, *A Nyoongar wordlist from the south-west of Western Australia,* Western Australian Museum, Perth.

Biskup, Peter 1973, *Not slaves not citizens: the Aboriginal problem in Western Australia 1898–1954,* University of Queensland Press, St Lucia.

Campbell, W.D. 1913, 'Description of a rock shelter with Aboriginal markings, and an indurated cast of a footprint at the Greenough River, and a cave dwelling at Narandagy Spring, Lockier River,' *The Journal of the Natural History and Science Society of Western Australia,* vol. v, pp. 10–14.

Carins, John 1977, 'The Wonggi's Lament', in Margaret Bull 1977, *Verse from the goldfields,* Hesperian Press, Victoria Park.

Curr, E.M. (ed.) 1887, *The Australian race,* Government Printer, Melbourne.

Curthoys, Ann 2003, 'Constructing national histories', in Bain Attwood & S.G. Foster (eds) *Frontier conflict: the Australian experience,* National Museum of Australia, Canberra, pp. 196–197.

Dictionary.com n.d., 'gnamma hole', *Dictionary.com Unabridged,* viewed on 18 April 2011, <http://dictionary.reference.com/browse/gnamma hole>.

Douglas, W.H. 1973, 'The language of south-western Australia', *Journal of the Royal Society of Western Australia,* vol. 56, parts 1 and 2, pp. 48–50.

Elkin, A.P. 1977, *Aboriginal men of high degree,* University of Queensland Press, St Lucia.

Equal Opportunity Tribunal 1997, *Substituted Note of Appeal*, 'On appeal from the Equal Opportunity Tribunal and in the matter of the Equal Opportunity Act (1984) WA and in the matter of a complaint by Joan Margaret Martin against the State Housing Commission', Supreme Court of Western Australia, Appeal Book Vol. 11997, 19 September 1997, p. 50.

Flood, Josephine 1995, *Archaeology of the Dreamtime: The story of prehistoric Australia and its people,* Angus & Robertson, Sydney.

Haebich, Anna 1992, *For their own good: Aborigines and government in the south west of Western Australia 1900–1940,* University of Western Australia, Nedlands.

Hallam, Sylvia 1975, *Fire and hearth: a study of Aboriginal usage and European usurpation in south-western Australia,* Australian Institute of Aboriginal Studies, Canberra.

Horton, David (ed.) 1994, *The Encyclopaedia of Aboriginal Australia: Aboriginal and Torres Strait Islander history, society and culture,* vol. 1, A–L, Aboriginal Studies Press, Canberra.

Howie-Willis, Ian 1994a, 'Amangu', in David Horton (ed.) 1994, *The Encyclopaedia of Aboriginal Australia: Aboriginal and Torres Strait Islander history, society and culture,* vol. 2, M–Z, Aboriginal Studies Press, Canberra, p. 45.

—— 1994b, 'Southwest Region', in David Horton (ed.) 1994, *The Encyclopaedia of Aboriginal Australia: Aboriginal and Torres Strait Islander history, society and culture,* vol. 2, M–Z, Aboriginal Studies Press, Canberra, pp. 1010–1012.

—— 1994c, 'Watjarri', in Horton, David (ed.) 1994, *The Encyclopaedia of Aboriginal Australia: Aboriginal and Torres Strait Islander history. society and culture,* vol. 2, M–Z, Aboriginal Studies Press, Canberra, p. 1162.

Inquirer & Commercial News 1865, 'Execution of native murderers of Bott at Butterabby on the 28th of January', 15 February 1865.

Isaacs, S. n.d., Native Vocabulary, Department of Land Administration, typescript.

Jutson, J.T. 1950, *The physiology (geomorphology) of Western Australia,* Government Printer, Perth.

Keeffe, Bert 1995, *Eastward ho: to Mullewa and the Murchison,* Mullewa Shire Council, Mullewa.

Landgate 2007a, 'History of Country Town Names', Former Department of Land Information, Government of Western Australia, Perth, viewed on 19 April 2011, < http://www.landgate.wa.gov.au/corporate.nsf/web/History+of+Country+Town+Names>.

—— 2007b, 'History of Metropolitan Suburb Names', Former Department of Land Information, Government of Western Australia, Perth, viewed on 19 April 2011, <http://www.landgate.wa.gov.au/corporate.nsf/web/History+of+metropolitan+suburb+names>.

—— 2007c, 'History of River Names', Former Department of Land Information, Government of Western Australia, Perth, viewed on 19 April 2011, <http://www.landgate.wa.gov.au/corporate.nsf/web/History+of+River+Names>.

Lodge, David 1992, *The art of fiction: illustrated from classic and modern texts,* Penguin, London.

Martin, Joan 2005, Album of artwork with commentary, interviewer and transcriber Jeanette Mellor.

Mickler, Steve 1997, 'The journalists' code of ethics and the Perth media's treatment of the Martin family eviction', viewed on 19 April 2011, <http://www.mcc.murdoch.edu.au/ReadingRoom/impi/articles/martins.html>.

Morris, Edward E. 1972, *A dictionary of Austral English*, Sydney University Press, Sydney.

Mulvaney, John & Kamminga, Johan 1999, *Prehistory of Australia*, Allen & Unwin, St Leonards.

Native Affairs 1933, 'Death of Tom Phillips on the 12 March 1933', Native Affairs file 54/27, 869/39 and 869/39.

Robertson, Beth M. 1996, *Oral history handbook*, Oral History Association of Australia Inc. (South Australian Branch), Openbook Publishers, Adelaide.

Salvado, Rosendo 1977, *The Salvado Memoirs: historical memoirs of Australia and particularly of the Benedictine Mission of New Norcia and of the habits and customs of the Australian natives*, trans./ed. E.J. Storman, University of Western Australia Press, Perth.

Tilbrook, Lois 1983, *Nyungar tradition: glimpses of Aborigines of south-western Australia 1829–1914*, University of Western Australia Press, Nedlands.

Tindale, Norman 1974, *Aboriginal tribes of Australia: their terrain, environmental controls, distribution, limits, and proper names*, ANU Press, Canberra.

UBD 1998, *Western Australia: State street directory cities and towns*, Universal Publishers Ltd, Osborne Park.

Wikipedia contributors 2011, 'Cordia', *Wikipedia, The Free Encyclopedia*, Wikimedia Foundation Inc., viewed on 19 April 2011, <http://en.wikipedia.org/wiki/Cordia>.

Wilkes, G.A. 1978, *A dictionary of Australian colloquialisms*, Sydney University Press, Sydney.

Wittenoom, F. n.d., *Memoirs of Murchison Pastoral Areas*, Geraldton Historical Society, Geraldton.

Index

Note: a page number in bold indicates an illustration.

Amangu (group) 18, 49
animals
  bardies (wood grubs) 58, 69
  bobtails 21, 68, 69
  bungarras (racehorse goannas) 21, 23, 66–8, 80, 81–2, 84–5, 91, 128–**9**
  bush turkey 65–6, 81
  dunarts (kangaroo mice) 54, 81–2
  emus 22–3, 65, 80, 81, 92–3, **130**
  kaguls (crows) 91, 92, 113
  lizards 66, 72, 85
  marrloo (red kangaroo) 22, 63, 64, 79–80, **124**
  ninghans (echidnas) 21, 47, 48, 64–5, 80
  nyiawls (mallee hens) 21
  snakes 19–20, 52–3, 68–9, 83–4, 89
art and craft 23, 42, 112, 113, 116, 144
  examples of author's paintings 117–30
  ground paintings 98, 115–16
  loss of paintings 113–14, 132
  and spirits / healing 91, 114–15
  see also cave paintings
artefacts 54, 59, 97, 102, 104
  disturbed or destroyed 59, 74–5
  as evidence of Aboriginal presence 48–9, 54, 56, 62, 66
  and sacred sites 77, 87
ashes 7, 63
  for cooking 22, 24, 65

Badimaia people/language 50, 51, 142
Beemarra 51–53, 78–9, 84–5, **129**
  SEE ALSO sacred sites, spiritual beliefs

bush medicine 23, 53, 69, 70–2

cave paintings 56–7, 73, 95, 96, 119, 149–150
  line cutters 57, 68
  see also rock shelters
caves 74–5, 95–7
Chookenau, Charlie 5–6
circumcision 18, 50, 97
  SEE ALSO corroboree, initiation, law
Coalseam 9, 12, 13, 18, 73, 157
corroboree 105–6, 109
  grounds 57, 72, 76–7, 102, 118
  SEE ALSO circumcision, initiation, law
Cue 1, 38, 48, 49, 51, 74, 95, 118

discrimination 3, 16, 33
  and land tenure 10, 47–8
  SEE ALSO homelessness, police
Dongara 1, 18, 21, 46–7, 49, 50, 149
Dreaming 12, 78, 83–4, 96–7
  depicted in paintings 118, **119**, 120–1, **120**, 130, **130**
  Rainbow Snake 53, 79
  tracks 49–56, 58, 78, 79, 110
  see also Beemarra, spirits

eviction 132–37
  SEE ALSO homelessness, housing

fire, traditional uses of 22, 39, 62–3, 101
  in Dreaming stories 83, 120
Follow the Rabbit-Proof Fence 26–7

Geraldton 40, 43, 49, 50, 106, 140, 148, 150
Ginny (Jenny) of Irwin 2, 5, 6, 11, 12,
government 13, 16, 47–8, 58–60, 89, 132–6
　and displacement of Aboriginal people 10, 17, 49
　SEE ALSO mining, Native Title, police

Hames, Dr Kim 137
Harris, Eva (*née* Phillips) 6, 7, 14, 27, 37, 76, 77, 93–4
　guidance by 21, 30, 39
Harris, Norm, Senior 9, 11, 14–5, 16, 25, 73, 77
　guidance by 8, 10, 14, 21, 30, 34–5, 39, 41
　loss of land 47–8
homelessness 42, 43, 113, 137–40
　growing up 19, 30–1, 33
　and Homeswest 133, 137–40
　SEE ALSO housing
Homeswest 132–6
housing 19, 23–4, 132–40

illness 3, 103, 104–5, 131, 140–2
　and bush medicine 23, 53, 69, 70–2
　in childhood 32, 40
　diabetes 35, 40, 138
　hereditary 34–5, 40
　and homelessness 137–9
initiation 16, 50, 105–6, 110–1
　see also circumcision, corroboree, law
Irwin River 1, 2, 13, 49, 149, 150, 151

Kangaroo Cave 95–7
Karalundi Mission 37
Koolanooka 19, 24, 101–2, 151

Lake Darlot 1, 47, 48, 79
land claims 10, 17, 50, 52, 59, 87, 118
　and author's claim 87, 143–4
　see also Native Title

law, traditional 2, 18, 56, 62, 100–1, 104–11, 76
　and food prohibitions 21, 27, 67
　law men 3, 4, 34, 48, 95, 104, 122
　and punishment 5–6
　responsibilities under 8–9, 44, 50
　and sacred / special sites 54, 75, 97, 100
　and skin names 1, 16, 53
　women's 76, 96–7, 102–03, 104, 121–2
　see also circumcision, corroboree, initiation
Lewis, Jane Margaret 'Wogera' (*née* Phillips) 1, 6–7, 14, 15
Little, Michael (Mick) 73, 74, 112, 114, 115

Mabo, Eddie 116–8, **117**
Martin, Dean 38, 132, 134, 135, 145, 146
Martin, Errol 38, 39, 43–4, 82, 135, 139
Martin, Greg 38, 57, 74, 113, 115, 132, 136
Martin, Jennifer (Jenny) 38, 40, 115, 132, 133, 134, 135, 138, 142
Martin, Leonard (Lennie) 35, 41, 42, 72, 91
Martin, Nicola (Nicky) 39, 43, 106, 134, 135, 141, 145
Martin, Sandra 39, 42–3
Martin, Stephen 39, 42–3
Mingenew 3, 12, 13, 18, 21, 47, 151
mining 55, 58–60, 98, 99, 102
　and destruction of Aboriginal sites 13, 52, 59, 60
　ecological effects of 82, 103
　and Native Title 58–60
　site clearance for 7, 59, 88, 97, 99, 102, 143
moban 82, 86, 87, 96
Moore River Settlement 5–6, 16–8, 37, 101

Index

effects on those incarcerated 1, 9, 17, 34
Morawa 1, 3, 8, 10, 19, 23–4, 29–33, 43, 47, 89, 150–1, 152–3
Mount Gibson 53–4, 77–8, 79, 82
Mount Magnet 3, 10, 33, 35–8, 39–40, 43–4, 151, 152–153
Mullewa 16, 29, 46, 149, 150, 151, 152–3

Narandagy 12, 14, 149–50
Native Title 46, 60, 112
    and influence of mining 58–60
    researching history for 2, 5, 6–7, 46, 132–33
    SEE ALSO land claims
Native Welfare, official records 3–4, 5, 7, 12, 13
    SEE ALSO removal of children, Welfare
New Norcia (mission) 37
ngalanggu (men who been through the law) 34, 122
    SEE ALSO law
Noongars (people) 45, 87, 92, 95, 129

ochre *see wilgi*

Paynes Find 43, 48, 49, 67, 77, 93–4, 100, 152–3
Perenjori 151, 153, 155
Perth 10, 30–1, 32, 35, 43, 45, 58, 70, 132, 133–4
Phillips, Amy (*née* Cameron) 1, 5–6, 10, 11, 14, 16
Phillips, Tom, Junior (Ullamarra) (grandfather) 2–3, 4, 5–6, 7, 15, 16, 47, 68
Phillips, Tom, Senior (great grandfather) 2, 3–4, 5
Phillips, Tom (uncle) 3, 7, 76, 95, 100
police 8, 16, 106, 107, 108–9, 132, 139
    black trackers 3
    and death of granddaughter 135–6
    historical files 46–7, 49

Rainbow Snake 51, 52–3, 78–9, **129**
    see also Beemarra
removal of children 5, 7, 16–17, 37, 42
    threats of 15, 24, 29, 40
    see also Moore River Settlement, Welfare
rituals *see* ashes, circumcision, corroboree, initiation, law
rock shelters 55–6, 73, 74–5, 201, 149
    see also cave paintings
Roelands Mission 36

sacred sites 13, 54, 55, 57, 67
    artefacts at 61, 87, 97
    checking of by lawmen 3, 5, 49, 68
    and Dreaming 11, 51, 53, 95–6
    and mining 13, 55, 60, 101–2
    and Native Title 97
    and ochre 89, 113
    spiritual sense of 40, 91, 98–100, 118
    and waterholes 46, 54, 55, 57
    women's sites 102–3
    and *wudatjis* 101
    SEE ALSO *wilgi*
salt, dietary laws 22, 64
sickness SEE illness
Sister Kate's (children's home) 17
spirits 4, 55, 86, 94, 124, 128–9
    of ancestors 4, 20, 59, 132
    and healing 72, 114–5
    expressed through painting **117**, 122, 124, **121**, **127**, 128, **129**
    as messengers and guides 41, 86, 87, 88, 100, 103, 118, 142
    wudatjis 101–2
spiritual beliefs 51–2, 78, 93, 94, 100, 115, 141, 142, 178
    and Christian beliefs 51–2, 53, 78, 79, 95, 141
    SEE ALSO Beemarra, sacred sites

Tardun Mission 29
Teaching Stones 74–5
    SEE ALSO artefacts

Tindale, Norman 18, 49, 87
totems 16, 34, 78, 89, 130
Wadjari people/country 51, 79, 118
Wageral people/country 2, 6–7, 14, 45, 46, 47
Wagyl 53, 79, 85, **129**
  SEE ALSO Beemarra
Welfare 6, 24, 29, 37, 40, 42, 109
  see also Native Welfare, removal of children
Widi 3, 7, 13, 14, 27, 37, 87
  country 18, 34, 48–50, 59, 67, 77, 79

Mob 1, 4, 45, 46–7, 48–50, 53
wilgi (ochre) 74, 79–80, 81–2, 84, 88–9, 95–6, 105, 113
wind, as spiritual force 98–9, 103, 115
Wongi people/country 22, 45, 79, 95
wudatjis (little people) 101–2, 126, **127**, 139

Yakabindie 53, 78–9
Yalgoo 43, 73, 99–100, 102
yamatji (friend) 45
Yamatji people/country 45–6, 51, 70, 118, **129**